Architecture of the World

Henri Stierlin

Mayan

Photos: Henri Stierlin
Preface: Pedro Ramirez Vazquez

Benedikt Taschen

Editor of series   Henri Stierlin
Plans   Georges Berthoud EPF SIA

Editor of English edition   Kenneth Martin Leake

Contents

Influence of the Maya on Contemporary Mexican Architecture

by Pedro Ramirez Vazquez

Whenever man encounters the remains of ancient civilizations and recognizes in them features which still prevail in contemporary culture he must feel a sense of wonder. This wonder is the greater when, as in the case of Mayan architecture and the architecture of Mexico today, there has been no natural historical sequence. For Mayan culture was suspended in time, mysteriously and abruptly cut off from all continuity with contemporary Mexican culture. But since all the pre-Columbian indigenous cultures of Mexico had many common characteristics, doubtless produced by an accumulation of similar influences, it is hardly surprising that many features common to Mayan culture should still survive today. And certain of these influences are inherent in nature itself: the landscape, the topography and the climate. None of these have changed over the centuries.

The contemporary Mexican reacts towards his climate and landscape in precisely the same way as did the Maya. The structure of the land remains unchanged and the land itself continues to yield the same building materials. With the development of modern building techniques these can now be used more profitably, but at the same time, the slow progress of local craftsmanship has kept alive both primitive tools and methods of working. And it is through this very craftsmanship and the rooted customs of local family life that the traditions of popular architecture, still preserved in the rural areas of the country, have been maintained.

The features of Mayan architecture which reappear most frequently in Mexican architecture and town-planning today, are the use of color, texture, and a generous sense of open space. A brief look at Mayan and other indigenous styles clearly shows the importance of the first two of these, color and texture. They are equally evident in the period of Spanish domination and in contemporary architecture.

University of Mexico: Tower block of the Rectorial
Building in the University City

The use of color has always been determined
by the Mexican landscape, and the use of
texture by a native sensitivity to the inherent
plasticity of the natural building materials
whose richness matches that of the landscape.
These have been permanent assets to Mexican
architecture from pre-Columbian times to the
present day. At the same time they have
always embodied the social influences of the
times: for instance the neo-classicism which
invaded the world in the nineteenth century,
and the functionalism in contemporary architecture, brought to life by the hesitations and
indecisions of our own century. Although they
have not reached the remarkable heights
achieved by Mayan buildings at Uxmal, Chichen,
Tikal, etc., contemporary Mexican architects
have always endeavored to maintain these
same high standards in their use of color and

texture, and at the same time to integrate both
painting and sculpture into their work.

The most important idea in contemporary
Mexican architecture is, without doubt, the
concept of open space. In fact in all indigenous
Mexican cultures, open space in town-planning
has always been used liberally, the groups of
buildings being fully integrated with their
natural setting. At Teotihuacan the simplicity
and starkness of the buildings blend perfectly
with the inhospitality of the landscape surrounding them, and the lushness of the jungle
concealing and imprisoning the remains of the
architecture of the Maya is complemented by the
richness of its dimensions and ornamentation.

This generosity in the treatment of open
space was determined by a profound respect for
the Mexican landscape, a sensitivity to natural
environment and by the desire to become a part
of this environment rather than to introduce any
foreign element into it.

In this way the great structures at
Teotihuacan, Sempoala, Monte Alban,
Tenochtitlan and more particularly the buildings
at the Mayan sites have become an integral part
of nature, so much so that it is no longer
possible to imagine these sites as they must have
been before the buildings existed. Not only did
they have this respect for their landscape and
the desire to blend their architecture with it, but
they had, too, a wonderful concept of human
scale and the heights of dignity which man can
reach through collective action.

This feeling for the importance of man so
manifest in the great open spaces of
Teotihuacan, in the Calzada de los Muertos, in
the square at Monte Alban, and in Mayan
architecture at Tikal, can only be explained in
this way, since the needs of modern traffic did
not concern the architects of the time. They

were motivated solely by their regard for human dignity and for the great numbers who were to congregate in these spaces; for even on religious occasions respect was equally apportioned between man and god. The gods were placed on a vertical plane and man on a horizontal plane: the gods in the heights of the temples placed as close as possible to the heavens, and man in his great congregations on the ground chained to the earth where he belonged.

Under Spanish domination in the sixteenth and seventeenth centuries Mexico began to see new urban developments and new architectural work. The native feeling for landscape and building materials and the survival of certain aspects of the collective organization of Mexican architecture, ensured that the traditional feeling for open space remained, and there evolved such typically Mexican solutions as the "open chapels". But slowly, indigenous architecture began to absorb and even accept European influence, particularly in its public squares, the European origins of which offered a link with the new type of collective life imposed by the Conquistadors.

It was the Conquistadors who enclosed the cities of Mexico in webs of narrow streets and alleys which, with their ornate façades in various styles, soon ousted the native architecture. Only after the 1910 revolution, when Mexico was confronted once more with her cultural origins, was there a revival of the three constants of color, texture and space.

Many different contemporary structures demonstrate this; in particular those at University City, where the architects, Mario Pani and Enrique del Moral, have created a clear

Faculty of Philosophy and Letters

harmony of proportion in the way in which they have linked the man-made open spaces with the natural environment. In the sports stadia at University City, Carlos Lazo, Alberto T. Arai, and Augusto Perez Palacios have achieved in their architectural forms the same participation in the landscape as did their pre-Columbian ancestors. In other buildings of University City various architects have tried to marry the texture and color of the natural building materials with the traditionally-inspired color and texture of the great murals.

Although this has been more successful in some cases than in others, it demonstrates at least the eagerness and inherent desire of Mexican architects to maintain this constancy in their work.

In Mayan architecture, in order to make open

Open spaces abound

space an integral part of the structure itself, three different solutions were used: courtyards, squares and quadrangles.

The courtyard was created by a mass of buildings irregularly placed, defining a small, open, but private, space. This has survived through the original Mediterranean courtyard introduced by the Spaniards.

The square, common to architecture and town-planning in all cultures, consisted of a larger open space, more public in character, not always regular in shape, which was limited not only by buildings, but also (and this is its most interesting feature) by platforms at various levels. It was always designed to be used by large assemblies of people.

The quadrangle, typical of Mayan architecture north of Yucatan, falls somewhere between the courtyard and the square. It was a small open space with buildings on all four sides, the quadrangles being linked to each other by openings in the buildings forming the corners.

Even today it is unusual to find such neat solutions to the problems of organizing open areas, whereby they are linked to each other by means of platforms at various levels, dispensing with the necessity for streets.

At its best Mayan architecture demonstrated a constructive power and an exquisite sense of form achieved by means of the neat proportions of its architectural elements, decorative details, sculptured reliefs and painted murals. Using only stucco and limestone these were handled in a variety of ways, sometimes being worked irregularly and sometimes in rectangles tending towards the square, with variable inlays. In most cases the horizontal joints were made continuous, the ashlars where they formed part of the ornamentation were treated as rectangles in

The Library: the windowless facades with their rich
polychrome decoration recall pre-Columbian art

which an angle is avoided, and corners were
rounded in order to emphasize the curve, imposing an almost calligraphic character, still to
be seen in popular architecture and in the
clothing of the present-day inhabitants of
Yucatan. This ornamental treatment is still
perfectly in keeping with the natural environment of the buildings.

In the door jambs, in the corners and in the
moldings, each architectural element was
formed by individual stones, and a notable
feature in the more complete Mayan sites,
Uxmal for example, is the fact that each stone
was in itself independent of the ornamentation
of the unit of which it formed part.

To put it in contemporary terms, Mayan
architecture was in its basic construction and
ornamentation a prefabricated architecture

which demanded a definite pre-conception and design, an organized and systematic manufacture, an orderly production and a methodical system of mounting and placing, since in no other way could its marvellous sculptural ornamentation be conceived. It was mass production determined by conditions which still survive today: an abundance of high quality labor, a collective organization with a high sense of discipline, and a respect for technical direction.

The lesson of Mayan architecture for contemporary Mexican architects is not limited to its aesthetic value but lies also in its rigorous technical accuracy, a prerequisite for the creation of beauty. The inspiration which Mayan architecture holds for the architect today becomes even greater after analyzing the harmonious way in which its integral elements are related. It does not matter which trend he might choose to follow: functional, organic, traditional or even international, with all of these the Mexican architect can enrich the natural color, texture and amplitude of space which are his heritage. He need not consciously return to his native architectural roots, since in the landscape, topography and cultural traditions of his country and in modern technique, he has all the elements necessary to give form to the space which the contemporary Mexican needs in order to live.

Mexico,

December, 1963.

8

First Contact with the Mayan World

The buildings left by the Mayan civilization inspire the onlooker with a sense of amazement, admiration and lyrical exaltation. There is a deeply-moving paradox between the clean-cut lines of this vast, powerful architecture, with its colossal pyramids and palaces of astonishingly modern horizontality, and the total hostility of its surroundings. The inextricable tangle of forest and undergrowth all but overwhelms the enormous monuments.

The jungle is a thick mantle over this great, flat, unchanging country of Central America. Above the horizons of the Peten and Yucatan pure white banks of clouds drive ceaselessly across the deep blue tropical sky. Below there are billows of another kind: branches of cedars and acacias, shrouded in creepers and blossoming lianas, often climbing to heights of a hundred feet and more.

Tree trunks rot in the humidity and, in spite of the chatter of birds, a heavy silence hangs over the great stone buildings. The few monuments that here and there manage to penetrate the greenery appear even more vulnerable to the constant assault of the forest.

It seems unlikely that any civilization could develop in such surroundings. Indeed, these cities, drowned in the interminable waving foliage, pose a multiplicity of problems. Who were the men who built them? When did they live? How were they able to create their magnificent civilization in this green hell? Why did so high a level of civilization simply vanish?

Survivals

The present-day descendants of the great Mayan builders seem to have forgotten their glorious past. The Maya still exist and the many centuries of foreign occupation following on the Spanish conquest have not extinguished their native pride and nobility. They still speak their own language, and continue to live according to their ancient customs and traditions, inhabiting huts of pisé and thatch as did their ancestors some two thousand years earlier.

The villages are composed of typical oval dwellings, their wattled walls covered in pisé whitened with lime. With their single door set in

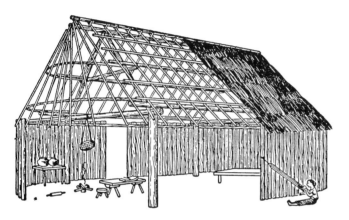

A present-day Yucatec hut with walls of wattle and thatched roof (after Thompson)

the center of one wall and their two-sided thatched roofs, they still resemble the huts portrayed in the sculptured friezes of the Mayan palaces.

Universal cleanliness bears witness to the highly-developed social sense of these people. Each house has a brilliantly green garden, carefully kept and surrounded by a dry stone wall. The inhabitants do their cooking out of doors beneath a lean-to, over-shadowed by lofty palms.

Today, even though the silhouette of a pink, rough-cast Baroque church with a bell-tower surmounted by a wrought-iron cross dominates the village, the Maya live in a world resembling that of their ancestors. Their settlements can be

mistaken for those that once surrounded the vast stone cities, the pyramids and temples of the ancient capitals. Only the nobles, the high priests and learned men who directed the ancient workshops have vanished. One cannot help wondering what faith animated this people—a faith that inspired them to build the hundreds of gigantic temples and countless cities strewn over Mayan territory.

Discovery

For three centuries after the Spanish conquest, the past was completely forgotten. The work of a Franciscan, Diego de Landa, which describes the Indians during the period of the Spanish penetration into Yucatan, remained unknown until 1863. The publication of de Landa's work, a century ago, coincided with a major research movement. Indeed, since the early nineteenth century, white travelers had been setting out to discover the ancient native cultures, memories of which were enshrined in legend. Humboldt, Kingsborough, Stephens, Bernouilli and, finally, Maudslay, gradually laid the foundations of pre-Columbian history.

The ruins of the Mayan monuments were testimony to the drama played out in the virgin forest nearly a thousand years before. Temples had been invaded by vegetation, towers were totally covered with creepers, pyramids split by the upward thrust of gigantic trees; reliefs had been prized off by roots, decorative work crumbled, plaster peeled off; flights of steps had been overturned, walls cracked; vaults had caved in and monoliths collapsed. Such sights were everywhere to be seen through a dense cloak of greenery.

Yucatan, Guatemala and Honduras still conceal many such undiscovered ruins. There are literally hundreds of ancient Mayan cities sleeping beneath their forest shroud still unknown to scholars and explorers. Each trek into the heart

Stele B from Copan, as it was discovered in 1840 by the explorer Stephens; after a sketch by Catherwood

of Quintana Roo reveals new ruins; each scientific expedition along the Usumacinta brings to light countless buildings to be cleared, studied and preserved from otherwise inevitable natural annihilation.

For this reason it is still too early to establish a complete list of treasures concealed in the great Mayan forests. Nevertheless, the vast number of buildings leads us to suppose that this region of Central America once ranked among the most highly populated areas of the world. Yet its golden age lasted for scarcely more than five centuries, and only a few regions such as Yucatan are still inhabited today.

Archaeological Works

The only people to have crossed these vast, hostile areas have been oil prospectors, chicleros and, for the past hundred years, archaeologists, who have attempted to bring the forgotten ancient capitals back to a semblance of their former glory. The work of these modern scholars has been on an immense scale, and in some cases they have been able to recreate almost intact the appearance of the sacred cities of the Maya.

We must consider how so perfect a reconstruction has been accomplished. There have been few ancient civilizations where it has been practicable to carry out similar reconstruction, for throughout the world, ancient buildings have been used, over the course of centuries, as quarries for new ones. The pyramids of Egypt were first stripped of their facings, then faced destruction by plunderers. Roman buildings were dismantled to build walls, and medieval churches vanished in lime-kilns. From earliest times, the custom of making fresh use of old materials has been consistently practised.

In Central America, in the land of the Maya, however, it was not so, for no new civilization arose to replace the extinct one. In forests which

Stele N from Copan; engraving after a sketch by Catherwood

even the natives could not master, no conqueror penetrated. The defeats suffered by the last free descendants of the builders of the Mayan classic period were those precipitated by the forces of nature. Only rarely were their lands occupied by strangers. Indeed, there is but one exception: a tribe of Mexican origin invaded northern Yucatan at the exact point where the deep forest turns to scrub. The invasion heralded a cultural renaissance by the Toltec-Maya, who established their capital at Chichen Itza. There are very few other sites where newcomers succeeded in introducing their own forms of worship, building their temples in a different style and substituting their own culture for that of the pure Maya.

The buildings of the classic period crumbled naturally. All the component parts survived and the archaeologists had only to set them up again in their original positions—though this was an extremely delicate task. The heaps of stones lying on the ground represent a larger-than-life jigsaw puzzle to the reconstruction experts. Architects need to replace what has been destroyed by the great forests. Stone mosaics and decorated walls are once more set in position, collapsed vaults and fallen columns are re-erected.

This skilled, scientific work is organized by the experts of the Mexican National Institute of Anthropology and History, and by American missions from the Peabody Museum, Tulane University and the Carnegie Institution of Washington. Restorations are limited to re-assembling the portions of shattered buildings; no new elements are added. Only the most slender margin for conjecture remains, and the completed work is remarkably authentic.

Mysteries and Hypotheses

Vast areas of the ancient Mayan territory remain unexplored. There are still countless mounds concealing half-destroyed buildings, and innumerable deserted cities, unknown even to the Indians, remain undisturbed in the jungle.

This break between past and present in Central America is both mysterious and disturbing. How did a nation succumb to the disappearance of all its leaders, the destruction of its élite, the obliteration of its literature and mathematics, and the complete eradication of its astronomy, a science in which it had become remarkably sophisticated?

These are some of the questions that puzzled the early discoverers of the Mayan masterpieces. A characteristic answer was that there was no connection between the Indians actually inhabiting the country and the ancient groups of architects and learned men. To those nineteenth-century explorers, it seemed impossible that the natives could ever have produced such a stupendous civilization.

The most preposterous theories were formu-

The upper temple of the Pyramid of Inscriptions at Palenque, overrun by the jungle (after Stephens)

lated, based on the idea that the great pre-Columbian civilizations originated outside America. Mayan culture was said to have come from Egypt, Israel, Greece or Scythia; or the Chinese or the people of South-east Asia were assumed to have introduced their civilization into the Western hemisphere before Columbus.

The authors support these theories of diffusion by pointing out similarities between the pyramids of Mexico and the ziggurats of Mesopotamia

Interior of the Temple of the Fine Relief at Palenque, at the time of Stephens' visit

which, with their raised temples linked to the ground by vast stairways, do bear a formal resemblance to the buildings of Central America. Other historians have emphasized likenesses between the hieroglyphics of the Maya and those of Crete and Egypt. These and other similar theories are the product of imagination, and their authors would have surpassed themselves still further had they anticipated the discovery by Alberto Ruz in 1952 of the crypt at Palenque. They might then have argued that since the Mayan pyramids concealed tombs similar to those found in Egypt in the time of the Pharaohs there was an undeniable connection between the two civilizations. In fact, such resemblances are superficial, and theories of this kind ignore historical and material data: they certainly do not prove the existence of contacts between civilizations separated by thousands of miles and thousands of years.

The most disturbing links, however, to which the exponents of diffusion have drawn attention, concern the cultures of South-east Asia. Between the temples of Palenque and the buildings of Angkor, for example, there are similarities: step pyramids, monumental flights of stairs, passages with corbeled vaults, a raised temple with porticoes, walls decorated with engaged balusters. Above all, there is a fundamental resemblance between the sites where these two almost contemporary civilizations flourished, for the jungle of Cambodia is as hostile as that of the Peten or Chiapas. The Khmers, along with the Maya, are among the few people to have achieved a high level of culture in virgin forests.

These are astonishing parallels, especially as it is now known that the population of America originally came from Asia.

In addition, as the works of Lévi-Strauss have stressed, certain stylistic similarities of symmetry and proportion are evident. The same

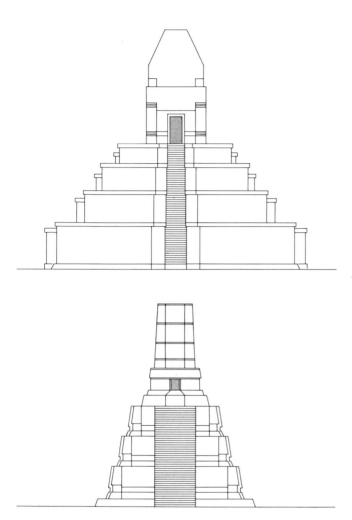

Similarities of structure: (a) Temple II at Tikal;
(b) The Baksei Chankrong at Angkor

The Unknown

The study of Mayan civilization induces caution, for there is little knowledge concerning it that can be positively substantiated by archaeologists and historians. Apart from certain mathematical and astronomical data, the texts of codices and lapidary inscriptions have not yet been deciphered.

Nor is there any definite chronology on which research workers agree. Despite intensive work on the subject and many scientific hypotheses (the most recent of which are based on the technique of Carbon 14 dating), no general agreement has yet been reached on the subject. The uses to which most of the buildings were put also remain unknown, and the decline and extinction of the Mayan civilization has still to be fully explained.

An Original Architecture

However many mysteries there may be regarding this great nation of builders, it can be incontestably affirmed that Mayan architecture has its own forms and laws. It is beyond doubt a form of original expression, with regional variations. Despite stylistic differences (to which we shall return later), it has a paramount sense of unity. Use is made everywhere of the same constituent parts: flights of steps, pyramids, masks as decorations for façades, corbeled vaults.

Mayan architecture is an art whose inspiration and aesthetic vigor, whose richness and refinement of ornament, whose nervous contrasts of light and shade remain unparalleled in history. One can discern a discipline of will imposed by man on nature, a type of absolute domination and implacable order. It would seem that the entire energy of the Maya was invested in their buildings, which they continually enlarged, decorated and refined.

decorative principles and graphic treatment of surfaces are found all around the Pacific basin, in archaic China, among the primitive peoples of Siberia and New Zealand, in Alaska, Melanesia —and in the lands of the Maya. The masks of Chinese bronzes, the totem poles of North America and the temples of Yucatan, decorated with masks of the god Chac, all bear witness to the same systematic formula.

The sense of power which springs from the vast esplanades and the artificial citadels, from whose summits buildings dominate the boundless forest, has its own feeling of lyricism. There is a sense of grandeur, hierarchy and geometry, revealing an aesthetic that is at once rational and superhuman. Some consider these creations overwhelming, oppressive and tyrannical; others are more sensitive to their pure dimensions, their broad scale and soaring rhythm.

Yet all experience awe and bewilderment when confronted with this civilization. Our terms of reference no longer apply. The basic structure of Central American civilizations is entirely different from ours, yet we must accept the fact that Mayan architecture has bequeathed to mankind unrivaled masterpieces. Its perfection proves that the laws of aesthetics played their full part even in a world whose basic criteria were different from our own.

Plates

Tikal (Guatemala)

21 **Small step pyramid** on the edge of the great plaza, close to Temple I. A staircase, preceded by several stelae, gives access to the summit of the building which lacks its upper temple.

22 **Temple I** to the east of the great plaza, seen from the summit of Temple II. Height of pyramid: 100 feet. Height of sanctuary with roof-comb: 56 feet. Total height: 156 feet. Right: detail of restored section, showing complex outline of steps and staging at the corners of the pyramid.

23 The steep staircase has no balustrade, but there is evidence of its having been widened and covered by steps which are now in a highly ruined state.

24 Side view of Temple I, showing massive roof-comb on the rear wall of the building.

25 **Wooden relief** (481 A.D.). This sculpture, 73 inches high and 82 inches wide, shows a Mayan divinity surrounded by fine inscriptions in hieroglyphic characters.

Copan (Honduras)

26 **The Ball-Court** (514 A.D.). The far end of the court is bounded by terraced steps surmounted by a stele; at the sides are inclined planes backed by vaulted buildings. In the right foreground is the hieroglyphic staircase with stele and altar in front.

27 Corbeled vault of the Ball-Court. This is a fairly rare example of this type of construction with the overhanging blocks still in position.

28 **The hieroglyphic staircase** (545 A.D.) takes its name from the text carved on the forward face of its 63 steps. The inscription consists of nearly 2,500 hieroglyphs.

29 Detail of decoration of side ramps.

30 Stele in high relief, known as Stele B (732 A.D.). A figure, richly clothed in ceremonial costume, is portrayed full face, fairly realistically, surrounded by elaborate decoration.

31 **The spectators' gallery** (762 A.D.). The wide flight of stairs of this name leads to a palace backing on the acropolis bordering the western plaza.

32 A statue in high relief, representing the storm god holding a torch.

33 Detail showing statue's integration with the architecture.

Palenque (Chiapas)

34 **The city** from the Temple of the Foliated Cross. Left: the Temple of the Sun. Right: the Great Palace, dominated by the Observatory tower.

36 **The Temple of the Sun** (642 A.D.) from the Temple of the Cross. Its mansard roof, decorated with stucco motifs, is topped by an openwork roof-comb.

37 **The Great Palace** and Pyramid of Inscriptions from the air. This view shows the artificial mound on which the Palace buildings stand.

38 The great courtyard from the second storey of the Tower. The roofs are ornamented with badly-damaged stucco motifs. On either side of the staircase are carved stelae.

39 Detail of sandstone stele on edge of staircase.

40 Vaulted corridor with portico supported by square pillars.

41 Detail of a hieroglyphic inscription in low relief found in the Great Palace, dating from 672 A.D.

42 **The Pyramid of Inscriptions** from the top of the Palace Tower. The porticoed sanctuary shelters an inscription dating from 692, from which the building takes its name. Height of pyramid and upper temple: 100 feet.

43 The vaulted funerary crypt discovered in the heart of the pyramid. A huge, sculptured limestone slab, weighing eight tons, covers the tomb of a priest-king.

44 View up the stairs leading to the crypt from the upper temple of the pyramid.

Map of Mayan territories

1 Dzibilchaltun
2 Acanceh
3 Yaxuna
4 Coba
5 Tulum
6 Edzna
7 Hochob
8 Uaxactun
9 Naranjo
10 Yaxchilan
11 Bonampak
12 Quirigua

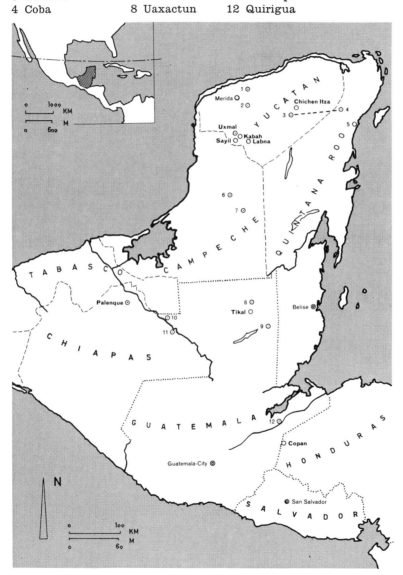

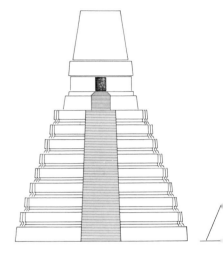

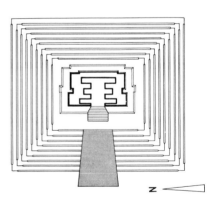

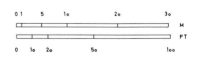

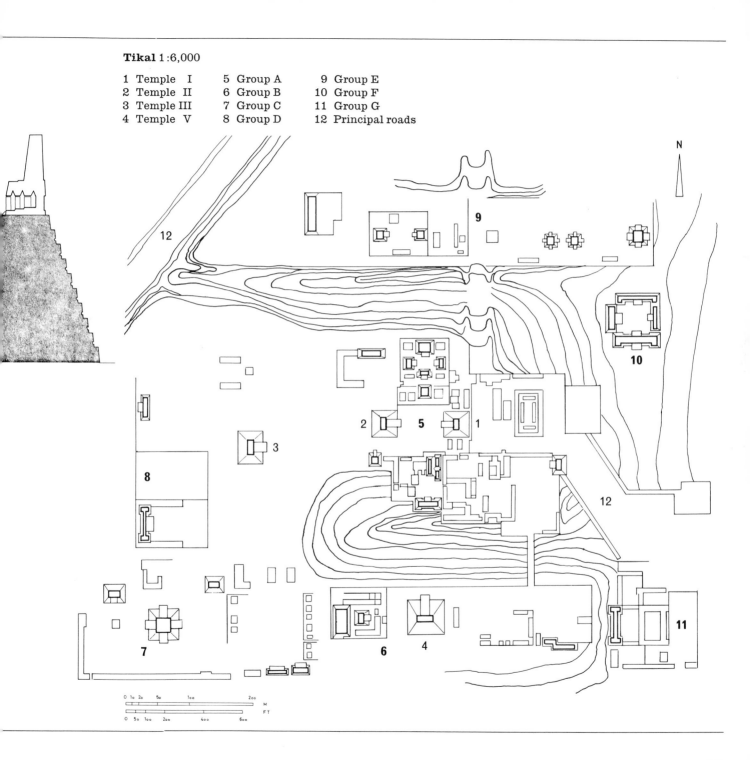

Tikal 1:6,000

1 Temple I	5 Group A	9 Group E
2 Temple II	6 Group B	10 Group F
3 Temple III	7 Group C	11 Group G
4 Temple V	8 Group D	12 Principal roads

N

12

9

10

2 5 1

3

8

12

7

6 4

11

O 1o 2o 5o 100 200
M
F T
O 5o 1oo 2oo 400 5oo

Notes

Tikal and the Peten

The sites in the south of the Mayan world, especially those of the region of the Peten, have been rediscovered fairly recently. It is less than a century since the earliest explorers ventured there. The great city of Tikal, for instance, was first visited by white men in 1877, when the Swiss, Gustav Bernouilli, came away with the famous bas-relief, now the pride of the Basle Museum.

These Mayan ruins were in a really catastrophic state: the jungle's destructive power had reduced most of the buildings to heaps of small stones. A few sculptures, however, gave an idea of the splendors resting beneath the shroud of green vegetation. The palaces and pyramids of the south are in a more ruinous state than those of Yucatan, not only because of the lofty forests of the Peten, but also because the monuments themselves are of greater age. The majority date from between the fourth and eighth centuries A.D., while the great buildings of the north rank between the seventh and ninth centuries and the so-called Mexican works were not erected until the twelfth century.

In Guatemala, English and American archaeologists have played a special part in research and restoration work. The Universities of Philadelphia, Tulane, Pennsylvania and Harvard, the Carnegie Institution of Washington, and the Peabody Museum have collaborated in this vast work and almost the entire Mexican contribution has been organized by the Ministry of Education and the Instituto Nacional de Antropologia e Historia (INAH), sometimes assisted by foreign scholars.

Reconstruction work in Mayan territory has necessitated virtual rebuilding. Only a few features may be left on the site and the original layout has to be rediscovered. This is what has recently happened at Tikal, where the architects entirely rebuilt some of the buildings, ranging from small pyramids to the colossal Temple I. Nevertheless, excavations and restorations are quite useless if they are not followed up by measures of conservation to guard against the humid climate of the country. The discovery of Pyramid E VII at Uaxactun, revealed in the course of a carefully organized series of excavations, was not succeeded by maintenance of the monument. This pyramid which was completely covered with magnificent stucco decoration was lost again within a few years.

Copan

The case of Copan is typical of the difficult problems encountered by the experts. In the course of time, the Copan river changed its course and began to eat away the artificial acropolis of the city; a large part of this had already been washed away before the arrival of the archaeologists. Their first task, before beginning their trial excavations, was to divert the river. There was, however, some compensation for the destruction that had taken place as the artificial hill now offered itself as a magnificent section one hundred feet high. Thus it was possible to determine its successive states and identify the buildings superimposed there in the course of the centuries.

Palenque

At Palenque the lofty foliage rising to a height of one hundred feet prevented any kind of overall view. The first travelers eagerly set fire to the forest to reveal the treasures that it concealed. These acts of vandalism could only accelerate the process of destruction, flaking off the damp stucco, breaking it up, and reheating the cement of the vaults. The trees which had loosened the stones also held them fast in their embrace; as soon as they died, the walls crumbled.

The discovery of the crypt of the Pyramid of Inscriptions by Alberto Ruz Lhuillier has been compared in importance to that of the tomb of Tutankhamen. He reached his goal in 1952 after four preliminary excavations. It was necessary to clear a vast vaulted staircase descending seventy feet into the heart of the pyramid from the upper platform. The staircase had been blocked to prevent access to the crypt, and when Ruz made a heavy, triangular stone door pivot on itself, he saw a great vaulted chamber in the middle of which was an enormous slab of carved limestone, six feet by ten feet, weighing eight tons. Beneath this slab was a sarcophagus containing the remains of a priest-king surrounded by a heap of jade ornaments, his face covered with a mosaic mask.

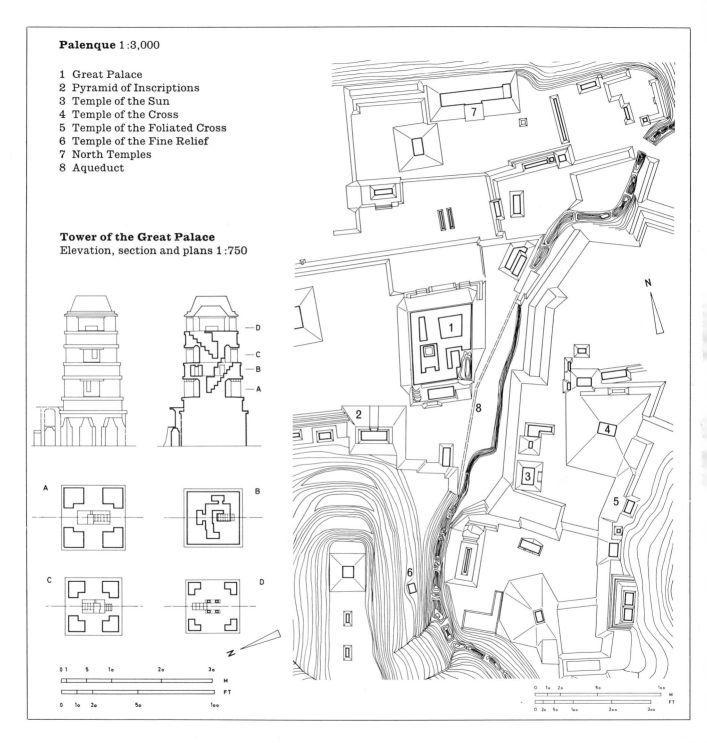

Palenque 1:3,000

1 Great Palace
2 Pyramid of Inscriptions
3 Temple of the Sun
4 Temple of the Cross
5 Temple of the Foliated Cross
6 Temple of the Fine Relief
7 North Temples
8 Aqueduct

Tower of the Great Palace
Elevation, section and plans 1:750

Pyramid of Inscriptions, Palenque
Elevation, section and plan 1:750

Crypt of the Pyramid of Inscriptions
Plan, section and elevation 1:200

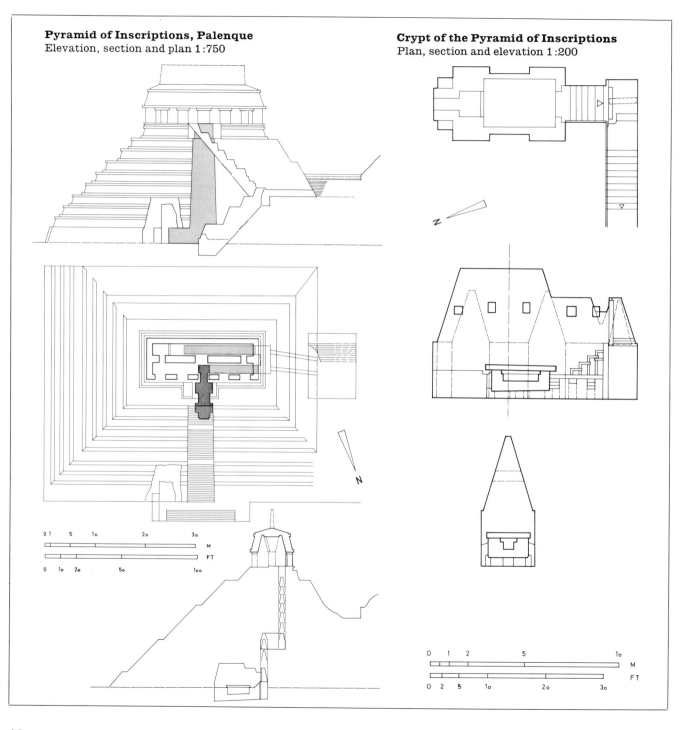

0 1   5   1o   2o   3o   M

0   1o   2o   5o   1oo   FT

0   1   2   5   1o   M

0   2   5   1o   2o   3o   FT

1. Background and Foundations of Culture

For an understanding of the origin and development of Mayan architecture, which in turn is governed by factors of geography, climate, techniques and religion, it is necessary to outline the foundations supporting the expansion of the most important culture of the pre-Columbian period—that of the Indians.

In America evolution followed completely different paths from those of the Old World. The background to its culture in no way resembles that of the great agrarian empires of the ancient world. There is no possible comparison between the plains irrigated at regular intervals by the flooding of great rivers such as the Nile, the Tigris, the Euphrates, the Indus and the Yellow River, and the lands of the Maya, where the soil covering is relatively thin and the rains frequently abundant.

It is not surprising that, in view of these differences, there existed agricultural techniques, food plants, and a social-economic system bearing no resemblance to those of Europe and Asia. For this reason, we must first touch briefly on the geographical setting in order to understand the sources of Mayan art and architecture.

Geography and geology

The territory of the Maya is situated in the heart of Central America in the extreme south of Mexico and extends over an area of about 125,000 square miles. It includes the present Mexican states of Yucatan, Campeche, Quintana Roo, Tabasco and parts of Chiapas, together with Guatemala, exclusive of the Pacific coast, British Honduras, the western fringe of Honduras, and a small portion of Salvador.

It is divided into three large provinces: in the south, the highlands of Guatemala, Honduras and Salvador; in the center, the great forest of the Peten, the basin of the Usumacinta and

Pasion rivers, and, finally, the completely flat lowlands of Yucatan.

To the north the peninsula of Yucatan is bordered by the Gulf of Mexico and to the east by the Caribbean. It lies at right angles to the lofty chain of volcanic mountains and is separated from the remainder of the continent by the isthmus of Tehuantepec and the Gulf of Honduras.

The main differences between the Mayan and Aztec regions lies in the proximity to the sea and coastal climate of the former, contrasted with the mountain harshness and violent differences of temperature prevailing in the latter. The other civilizations which arose in the swampy coastal plains directly bordering the Gulf of Mexico can be distinguished from the Mayan by the invading forest and scarcity of stone materials. The Mayan civilization was established in a region sufficiently flat to favor swift communication and sufficiently rich in freestone to provide materials for a monumental architecture: limestone of the tertiary age, often of a chalky quality, and always soft, formed the basic material for their great buildings. In addition to rocks rich in carbonate of lime, including lias and dolomite, the Maya discovered other stones in the southern portion of their territory: pink and white sandstone of paleozoic formation, volcanic andesite, the green trachyte of Copan, and hard flints which they used as tools. The mountainous region also furnished serpentine and jasper and the magnificent obsidian which the peoples of Central America carved and polished with such wonderful results. Quite recently deposits of jade have been discovered in Guatemala and banks of flint are scattered throughout the chalk country.

From the geological point of view Mayan territory, and particularly Yucatan, enjoys one other peculiarity—eroded limestone. In the pleistocene age, when vast masses of water were immobilized in the polar glaciers causing a considerable lowering of the level of the seas, Yucatan, with its humid climate and limestone formation, was in all probability transformed into a kind of strainer. Wells and pot-holes drained off the rain water into subterranean rivers probably a hundred feet below the surface of the limestone plateau. After the glacial period, when the level of the sea rose again, the whole tableland of Yucatan became buoyed up and these underground conduits were filled with water. The impressive wells which exist today are reminders of the former limestone watercourses which are now submerged.

Climate, flora and fauna

The Mayan territory is entirely situated south of the Tropic of Cancer, and so enjoys a warm, generally humid climate, except in the northern part of Yucatan where the rains are comparatively scanty. The entire region is swept by the trade winds which blow from east to west, causing the clouds to discharge as they follow the rise of the ground. The humidity in the atmosphere often exceeds 80 per cent.

In the south the typical vegetation is that of the great evergreen virgin forest where the trees rise to a height of 100 to 130 feet and tropical creepers flourish in the damp undergrowth. The chief species of trees are acacia, red cedar, sapodilla, rubber tree and palm.

Towards the north lies an intermediary zone where the trees are not so high and, finally, there is the low-lying forest of northern Yucatan where the vegetation is more like scrub.

The wild animals of the Mayan forest include jaguars, tapirs, deer, hogs, boars and monkeys. There is also a great variety of birds such as toucans, parrots and turkeys, all sizes of snakes and lizards, and a host of forest insects.

Thus the setting for Mayan civilization offers only limited riches. Though the stone is excellent, there are no underground resources apart from oil. Above all, there is an absence of minerals. The virgin forest is exceptionally difficult to cultivate, the soil is thin and soon exhausted. Why, then, was this region the cradle of the highest pre-Columbian civilization?

Origins of Population

Although anthropologists have for some time attributed an Asiatic origin to the people of the American continent, there is no evidence of the existence of man in North America earlier than 22,000 B.C. This is late; man's appearance in the Old World dates back between 600,000 and 1,000,000 years. Moreover, there is confirmation of the spread of Siberian elements in America in the paleolithic and mesolithic periods; these probably arrived by way of the Bering Straits. Asiatic tribes could have passed, almost unaware, from one continent to the other on a winter's hunting expedition, when the 80-mile strip of sea dividing them was frozen over.

Whatever connections there may have been with Asia must soon have ceased, probably at the end of the mesolithic period. Otherwise there would be no explanation for the characteristic lack of progress of the American continent in the fields of botany, zoology and technology. The contribution of the Asiatic population probably ended with their settlement at the beginning of the neolithic period and this was the exact moment when the first important signs of technological progress—domestication of animals, agriculture and pottery—began to appear.

Thus the Indians seem to have discovered everything for themselves, which theory would explain the homogeneity of the original pre-Columbian civilizations. For the basic conquests of the neolithic age revealed themselves simultaneously in North and South America.

The common bases of this development were largely conditioned by the supporting economic foundations which were everywhere the same, maize being the fundamental food plant in the New World, both in the uplands and in the lowlands. Thus the evolution of the Eurasian people, whose diet was basically one of rice and cereals that could be converted into bread, must not be confused with that of the Indian tribes. The profound originality of America lies in the fact that the continent produced a series of civilizations based on maize. According to the archaeologists there is evidence from excavation that maize was cultivated before the fifth millennium. The farmers of pre-Columbian America, however, were also familiar with such vegetables as beans and the calabash, and with various kinds of fruit. There are references also to cotton, tobacco, cocoa and medicinal herbs.

Their methods of cultivation were all founded on five to ten-year rotations. Everywhere it was necessary to clear areas for cultivation. When they had been exploited for a term of years and the harvests then diminished, the fields were abandoned, and the virgin forest quickly took back possession of the land.

Both animal and plant life in the American continent had a singular characteristic: numerous species, widespread elsewhere, were either absent or disappeared before the neolithic period. According to experts in prehistory, the horses and camels which frequented the lofty plateaux along with bison and mammoths became extinct around the sixth millennium. The reason for this is a mystery which paleontologists have been unable to solve. Whatever it may have been, the Indians inhabiting the north of the isthmus were familiar only with dogs, turkeys and bees, together with several species of llama.

Thus they could count only on their own physical strength for agricultural work and the transport of heavy materials.

Bases of Technology

The culture with which we are concerned was of the neolithic type, but offers surprising gaps. Although the Indians knew how to make pottery, they were unaware of the lathe or the wheel. Metalwork did not appear until well after its adoption by other great civilizations.

The common foundation of the pre-Columbian civilization can be placed between the second millennium and 500 B.C., at about which date emerged the cultures of Teotihuacan on the high Mexican plateaux and of Monte Alban further to the south in the region adjoining Chiapas. It is probable that the civilizing impulse sprang from the central plateau of Mexico, where the most ancient traces of religious buildings are found. We should remember the part played by the mysterious Olmec people further to the east on the coast of the Gulf. They too made rapid progress and may perhaps be considered the initiators of Mayan civilization, the origins of which go back to the last centuries before the birth of Christ. There are conflicting theories concerning the origin of the Mayan civilization, but it is certain that very early contacts existed between the two peoples across the region of Tabasco and that their relationship was not fortuitous.

Before the birth of Christ every center of early civilization saw the construction of cities with pyramids of pounded earth or stone; there were also statues and bas-reliefs, some of colossal size. Wall painting, too, came in with the megalithic period, heralding the first elements of a writing that was at first pictorial and later hieroglyphic.

In the world of the Maya, shortly before the beginning of the Christian era, complex buildings and impressive pyramids began to appear. Even in the heart of the virgin forest, tribes grouped themselves around vast religious centers. Uaxactun and Tikal, sacred cities dating from the third century, bear witness to a whole series of technical discoveries of primary importance—an architecture of masonry requiring cement and stucco; a system of decoration whose formal vocabulary became firmly established and, most important of all, a hieroglyphic writing which served to record the dates of a complex calendar based on a remarkably advanced form of mathematics and astronomy.

The engraved hieroglyphics of the first inscriptions recorded on stelae or jade are so precise that they must obviously be the result of long development and patient stylization. Texts which unfortunately could not have survived (having been recorded on perishable materials) must have existed several centuries earlier.

This writing deserves detailed examination, for it is of great importance in the dating of buildings. What is more, the Maya, unlike the South American Inca, were able to record facts in detail. This made possible the scientific expansion of their civilization, for figures and calculations are more difficult to transmit orally than poetry or rituals.

Writing

Mayan writing consists of almost 400 hieroglyphic signs found on stone stelae, wooden lintels, pottery and codices made from a kind of paper composed of vegetable fibres impregnated and covered with a fine coating of glazed lime. Research specialists have deciphered only between 150 and 200 of these signs.

Modern scholars have made it possible to decipher with certainty numbers, names of days, months and gods. But the Mayan vocabulary is not yet understood. The majority of the signs deciphered are ideographic, but we may also assume that some of the surviving hieroglyphics represent syllables. If the remaining signs were all ideographs, they would be insufficient to represent the thousands of words of a language, however limited it might be. Some of these hieroglyphics, therefore, must have been used, as in Egypt and Babylon, to denote sounds and not ideas.

Decipherment in Progress

A group of Soviet scientists has carried out an experiment endeavoring to solve the mystery which continues to surround Mayan writing.

The periodical review "Soviet Union", published in Moscow, recently stated that three young Siberian scientists, E. Evreinov, I. Kossarev and V. Oustinov, working under the direction of Professor Sobolev, Director of the Institute of Mathematics of the Siberian section of the Academy of Soviet Sciences, have succeeded in deciphering Mayan manuscripts with the aid of an electronic computor. Three codices called the Madrid, Dresden and Paris manuscripts and a few inscriptions engraved on stone constitute the only written documents of Mayan civilization. These manuscripts contain 372 hieroglyphics, 200 of which are still complete mysteries. The meaning of some of the other signs can be guessed through their shape—as in the case of the sun, the turkey and the fish.

The repetition of certain signs has led the Soviet scientists to believe that they represent prefixes or suffixes. By studying the regular construction of portions of phrases, entire phrases and groups of phrases, they have been able to isolate nouns of particular meaning.

This new development deserves comment. Until now we may agree with Paul Rivet that only a third of the Mayan signs have been identified. But if this decipherment by the

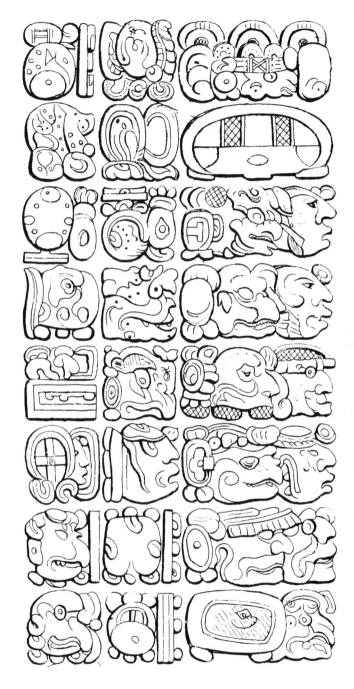

Detail of a Mayan hieroglyphic inscription found by Catherwood in the Temple of the Sun at Palenque

Russians is really accurate, it will constitute a revolution regarding our knowledge of the Mayan world, although the amount of information we shall gain by being able to read the texts will be limited. Any new interpretation, however, will lead to a better knowledge of the workings of the system of notation and linguistic and grammatical constructions. Above all it will enable us to learn the meanings of the dedicatory inscriptions of the stelae set up in front of Mayan buildings, and so make it possible for us to know the purpose for which they were used.

Although we are now able to read dates, concordance with our own chronology is not recognized by all the experts. Decipherment could be of use in identifying the people represented on the stelae. Similar information would be equally valuable as a basis for the investigation of the political-social system that regulated the Mayan world.

Mathematics and Decipherment

After World War I, a group of experts, by applying the statistical techniques used during the war for decoding secret messages, managed to establish a set of linguistic rules and to analyze the frequency rate of various grammatical constructions in a given language. Using such methods, Dhorme and Virolleaud, who had been attached to a decoding unit in the Dardenelles, succeeded in translating tablets written in the Giblitic and Ugarit languages. An electronic machine can facilitate and shorten such calculations, but this particular method can only be applied to a tongue belonging to a known family of languages. As varying Mayan dialects are still spoken by nearly two million Central American Indians, it is difficult to estimate the changes of idiom that have taken place over half a millennium and to determine the branch to which the surviving texts belong. As a result, new research must allow for a considerable margin of uncertainty.

Professor Sobolev describes the theoretical process of decipherment as follows: "To read the manuscripts, it is necessary to make successive comparisons of each hieroglyphic with each letter or word in the Mayan dictionary, to consider carefully all its possible meanings and choose the exact sense after comparing it with words already known. This series of operations, apart from any others, would require the analysis of every possible combination of the 200 given elements, and the amount of combinations would total a figure composed of 300 digits. No man, no electronic machine even, could achieve such a task."

Thus it was first necessary to reduce the field of research to a minimum, bringing forward other co-ordinates so as to cover the largest number of possibilities. The next step involved the analysis of recurrent combinations and a study of all those signs that appeared most frequently, in an attempt to identify them as prefixes or suffixes. The researches of the Russians at the Siberian Institute of Mathematics and those of Knorosov, another Russian engaged in decipherment, should not be under-estimated. Eventually they are bound to contribute to the solution of the riddle of the Maya.

The Texts

Apart from the great codices, our knowledge of Mayan literature is confined to a few works dating from after the Spanish conquest. They are prophetic and religious works, mingling magic and incantations with ancient chronicles. Because of the state of the texts, however, it is often difficult to disentangle Christian borrowings from the authentic elements. One of the texts of greatest interest to historians tells of the migrations of the tribes: "And they left, and arrived at a place called ...." These chronicles, which are probably linked with the widespread movement of populations which marked the advance of Mexican tribes into Mayan territory, have to a large extent served to support theories of migration and abandoned cities: in fact, they seem to relate to a period when the decadence of the Mayan world was already almost complete.

Arithmetical Knowledge

Mention has already been made of numbers among the decoded signs. Herein lies great promise for the archaeologists and historians. For the discovery of the meaning of these hieroglyphics is of primary importance for the understanding of the calendar, astronomy and chronology of the Maya. It makes it possible to read the dates on the stelae erected in the ancient cities of the Peten. The Mayan custom of giving dates to almost every architectural work, at least up to the end of the classic period, is of invaluable benefit to the historian.

Considerable research has resulted in the reading of the figures; it has provided valuable information regarding Mayan mathematics, which achieved a remarkably advanced level. Indeed it is in the sphere of mathematical calculation, the working out of volumes, proportions and angles, that the development of their architecture is explained. The quantities of materials and the organization of workshops were all regulated by mathematics. It is for this reason that the following brief account is appended.

The system is founded on a positional numeration based on the number 20. That is to say the Maya changed columns in twenties instead of tens as we do: their system changed in units of twenty, four hundred and eight thousand, instead of in tens, hundreds and thousands. The idea of zero is represented by the sign of a shell while one point marks one unit, two points two units, and so on. Five units are represented by a bar. There are also 19 signs for the first 19 numbers. With such means at their disposal the Maya were able to manipulate huge figures.

The ingenuity of this system can only be enhanced when we recall that we are dealing with a stone age culture. In these circumstances the invention of zero shows how far advanced their calculations were. For a major weakness of Graeco-Roman civilization, despite its superiority in the fields of technology, philosophy and science, lay precisely in its ignorance of positional mathematics and zero, which came to us from the Indians through the medium of Arab merchants.

Astronomy and the Calendar

Mayan mathematical knowledge was first applied to establishing a calendar. As in all civilizations based on agriculture, general prosperity depended on the marking out of the seasons. Without some form of astronomy, however primitive, there can be no calendar.

The Mayan priests evolved statistical methods, which were based on averages established by frequent observations over a very long period. These methods, together with the mathematical instrument at their disposal, enabled them to develop an amazingly valuable and exact type of

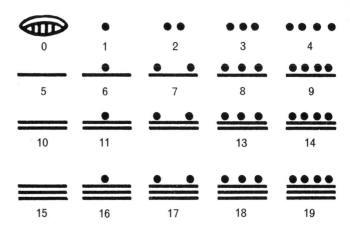

Mayan hieroglyphics representing numbers from 0 to 19

astronomy. At Palenque, Uaxactun, Chichen Itza and Mayapan are towers and groups of buildings considered by many experts to have been ancient observatories. We may wonder about the results of their calculations, for their knowledge profoundly influenced their architecture and some aspects of their town-planning.

The Mayan calendar was a complicated one, being based on threefold terms of reference: the solar year of 365 days on to which was grafted the religious year of 260 days, both being united in the Venus year which is the longest of the three, as the planet Venus accomplishes only five revolutions while the earth moves through eight solar years.

The Mayan solar year was broken up into 18 months of 20 days—again the system based on 20—at the end of which was added another period of five days. The periods of time covered by their calculations did not stop here. Twenty years of 360 days were a katun, and multiplication by 20 continued to form different cycles comparable to our centuries and millennia.

It is strange to find in this mathematical time scale that the Maya established an era. Just as the Christians fixed the start of their scale with the birth of Christ, the Mohammedans with the hegira and the Romans with the date of the foundation of Rome, so the Maya reckoned their chronology from the year 3113 B.C. The choice of this distant date is unexplained, for we know that the great period of Mayan civilization did not go back before the Christian era.

The marvels of the celestial mathematics of the Central American Indians become fully apparent when we study their lunar and venusian calendars. Here their calculations are based both on exact astronomical plans and a manipulation of figures which is truly astonishing.

The Dresden manuscript gives a total of 405 lunar months, computed at 11,960 days, whereas modern astronomers state that this period represents 11,959·088 days, which amounts to a displacement of one day every 380 years.

Similarly, with regard to the Venus-year and its multiples, the Maya based their calculations on a global period of 384 years and established the average revolution of Venus as equaling 584 days. Present-day experts fix it at 583·92 days. Such astronomical figures stress a high standard of precision, all the more amazing when we remember that they were the work of a neolithic people.

Methods of Reckoning

At this point we should consider how the Indians of the Peten who had no knowledge of the wheel or of metals, succeeded in obtaining such remarkable results. To work out the revolution of Venus with only a marginal error of just over an hour per year is a surprising achievement, especially if we think of the problems the Maya faced. We must realize first of all that they had no exact system of telling the time. They certainly had no water-clocks or hourglasses—devices which are, in any case, very inexact. Their technical resources must have been limited to lines of sight, calculations based on triangulation, and measurement of the distances cast by shadows.

The gnomon must have been the first means employed by our ancestors to determine the solstices, the longest and shortest days of the year. The gnomon was originally merely an upright stick from which the observer determined by measurement of its slanting shadow, at what moment of the year the sun was highest in the sky.

After the gnomon it is probable that the use of a primitive sundial enabled man to advance to an approximate form of time-telling. Time obtained by these methods remained inaccurate, however, because of the varying lengths of the days of the year and the imprecision resulting from the blurred edge of the shadow, caused by the width of the sun's diameter.

From the gnomon in its role of a vertical pole, we pass to the idea of sight-lines by means of which it is possible to site the position of the sun's rising at the times of solstice. It is necessary to find the northernmost point of its appearance in summer and the southernmost in winter. The same calculations, repeated at sunset, will provide the dates of the solstices.

For the Maya these sight alignments presented little difficulty, as the regions of Yucatan and the Peten are flat. Only the presence of clouds could sometimes prevent them from measuring certain phenomena over several weeks. When that happened they would be obliged to postpone their observations until the following year.

These sight-lines could equally well be obtained by means of long, narrow loopholes such as the openings in the upper chamber of the Caracol at Chichen Itza. Apart from such edifices, groups of buildings were constructed according to a given orientation, as at Uaxactun, where the sunrise on a certain day could be seen directly behind the corner of one building from the top of another.

Nocturnal Observations

Our next concern is the more complex form of astronomy dealing with the observation of the stars in the night sky. Here it is essential to bear in mind that the entire stellar structure of Mayan astronomy interprets visible movements only. They calculated the functions of the heavens as they seem to be, not as they are.

As far as the moon and the evaluation of its calendars were concerned, it was enough, in principle, to take into consideration a sufficiently large number of its cycles to work out the average duration of a complete cycle from one full moon to the next.

The problem becomes more complicated when it concerns the planets. Here, Venus was the chief concern of the Maya. Why Venus, we may ask, rather than any other planet? The reason would seem to be that the sight-lines for Venus are easier than for any other planet, though its course appears irregular.

Venus is visible before sunset and remains in the sky for a few minutes after dawn. Representing as it does, the passing of day into night and night into day, the planet is a symbol of resurrection in almost all mythologies, and is linked with the rites of every kind of passing in man's existence: birth, initiation and death.

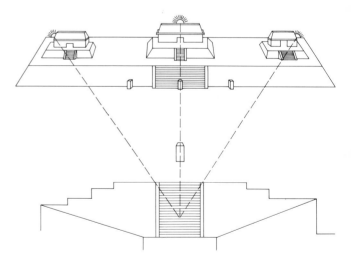

The observatory at Uaxactun: from the viewpoint of an observer on the steps of pyramid E VII, the sun appears within the left angle at the summer solstice, within the right angle at the winter solstice, and behind the centre temple at the equinox (after Ricketson and Morley)

It was this star which enabled the Maya to achieve the measurements of angles at a given moment, despite the absence of instruments capable of precise estimation of time intervals. They put their entire trust in simultaneous happenings: the height of Venus in the sky at sunrise or sunset permitted such calculations. Thus they succeeded in working out the apparent revolution of this planet—which lasts for over a year because of the rotation of the earth in the same direction in relation to the sun. Though, in actual fact, the real revolution, unknown to the Maya, lasts only 224 days, 7 hours.

The working out of angles between the sun and Venus at the moment of sunrise or sunset postulates the existence of some form of visual aid. Some simple form of equipment must have been used. There are, for example, the crossed sticks shown in some manuscripts; and at night they may have used a spider's thread stretched between two points and lit by a flame placed behind a screen away from the observer who thus had a sight-line, not blinding, yet visible even on the darkest night. Lastly, archaeologists have discovered in the lands of Central America peculiar jade tubes between 8 and 12 inches in length, whose use is still unexplained. These could perhaps be a crude form of astronomical telescope. These objects are similar to pieces of Chinese jade which have recently been identified as astronomical instruments. One can also assume the existence of a variety of wooden instruments which would have permitted the fixing of the tubes and the determination of triangulations.

The heavenly structure of the ancient Maya was never based on the clock, yet by simple calculations founded on the angles of shadows and the working out of coincidences and phases they achieved results of a remarkably high standard based on the law of averages. Calculations repeated a sufficient number of times

produced very satisfactory results. Indeed, according to one expert, the Mayan calendar is more accurate than the Gregorian, on which our own year is based. With the Maya, statistics corrected the findings of a relatively primitive astronomy and spatial geometry.

Thus, there seems to be no necessity to postulate unknown techniques in order to understand their astronomy, any more than there is need to

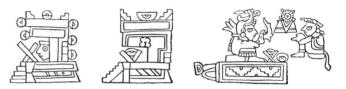

Representations of astronomers from Mexican codices: the observer uses two crossed sticks to take sight lines (after Morley)

have recourse to lost secrets to explain the building of their pyramids and palaces.

The Cult of Time

So much preoccupation with the calendar, the passage of time and the movement of the heavenly bodies betrays a philosophical-religious obsession. This seems to include the concept of linear time, especially as the Maya recognized the existence of an era. On the other hand, the ancient religion of the Central American peoples had never completely freed itself from the idea of an everlastingly recurrent time cycle, common to all primitive cultures. Thus Mayan chronology takes its place in a unity made up of vast cycles apparently extending over many millennia and eternally recurrent.

This philosophy of time based on the determination of certain astronomical dates whose sacred significance had to be commemorated by the erection of stelae and monuments, has provided archaeologists with a wonderful tool with which to discover the age of Mayan buildings.

This is not as simple as it sounds, however, for it is first necessary to learn to read chronological inscriptions whose system of writing includes special signs. Dates in the Mayan era are indicated by five figures: 9.17.0.0.0., for example. The first hieroglyphic represents the number of baktuns, one of which is equivalent to 144,000 days; the second indicates the katuns, each of which comprises 7,200 days; and the third, the tuns, periods of 360 days; the fourth corresponds to the 20-day month— uinal—and the last to the kines or days.

It was undoubtedly difficult to get to know the mechanism of this complicated, yet rational, reference system, but we are faced with a more difficult problem when we try to work out the starting point of the Mayan era in relation to our own and to find a concordance between the Mayan and the Gregorian calendars. The theories of those adhering to a long, and those supporting a short, chronology, have for long been in opposition. Differences can amount to as much as three centuries, according to whether one uses the method adopted by Spinden, or that of Goodman-Martinez and Thompson. So far the latter has come off better in relation to datings worked out with the aid of the Carbon 14 technique, though we must realize that even the most modern scientific methods cannot provide us with absolute certainties: a margin of error of 100 to 150 years when dealing with periods of 1,500 years is still a considerable handicap.

It is Thompson's chronology, however, which admits the greatest likelihood. For this reason, we have in this book made basic use of his calculations, with which the foremost experts are beginning to agree. Nevertheless the fluid state of our knowledge on this subject must be borne in mind; the latest technical publications continue to question acknowledged dates.

In any event, such adjustments are necessary to prevent erroneous theories from becoming accepted. A particular example of this is the almost total abandonment of Morley's ideas for a chronology which were incorrectly based on a series of dates appearing in the late chronicles. These gave rise to extraordinary legends concerning Mayan civilization. Now his famous distinction between the Old and New Empires is no longer accepted. He believed that several centuries divided the creations of the regions of the Peten, Copan and Usumacinta from those of Yucatan. He quite rightly placed the former between the fourth and eighth centuries A.D., but thought they were then followed by a wide gap marked by a total absence of artistic, architectural and cultural production. The progress of Mayan civilization was then resumed, but in the northern part of the country only. In order to explain this phenomenon Morley spoke of the abandonment of the cities of the Old Empire, situated in the southern regions, and the migration of the entire Mayan population towards the north. Cultural activities were not resumed until two centuries later under the New Empire. This theory also postulated changes in climate and other factors such as epidemics and the exhaustion of the soil.

Mayan Art in Two Provinces

In fact, the two regions of the Mayan world came into being almost simultaneously, as has been convincingly proved by the recent excavations at Dzibilchaltun. Though they can be distinguished by stylistic differences, there is no break separating a classic period from a late renaissance. On the contrary, archaeologists have proved that the earliest dates in both provinces are parallel in time. In Yucatan stelae have been found going back to A.D. 415, while at Tikal the first known dates are around A.D. 300.

Though we may disregard the distinction

between the Old and the New Empires, it appears that differences between the northern and southern provinces have an important part to play. Here we are concerned with two closely-linked regions rooted in the same civilization; the emergence of the Peten, however, took place between the fourth and eighth centuries, while the creations of Yucatan did not bloom fully until some time between the seventh and ninth centuries.

Thus, despite there being only one kind of writing and what seems to have been a common religion, appreciable differences seem to have continued to exist between the various members of the Mayan federation. Nowhere does there emerge a picture of a centralized kingdom or a unifying power. On the contrary, even more than in ancient Greece, the Mayan world gives the impression of a loose union of small religious principalities which flowered at definite dates. At a time when the city of Copan and the valley of the Usumacinta in the region formed by the Peten had already sunk into decadence, Yucatan was at the height of its architectural splendor.

Furthermore, the differences between the northern and southern provinces rest on the existence of a language barrier, traces of which still survive today. Whereas the characteristic homogeneity of the north was founded on the Yucatec language, the southern region was split up into several dialects springing from the same family. Or perhaps the simple explanation is that Yucatec remained more vigorous and succeeded in making inroads into the region of the Peten, whose Indian population has now almost completely disappeared.

We shall see that the chief architectural disparities between north and south are distinguished by easily differentiated styles. There is a relative unity throughout the Yucatec region despite the existence of three styles called by archaeologists Chenes, Rio Bec and Puuc; in the south, too, there are well-defined modes of expression in the three regions already mentioned—those of the Peten, Copan and Usumacinta.

Mexican Revival

Finally, it must be remembered that a real renaissance took place in the north of Yucatan with the arrival of the Itzas, a tribe of Mexican origin. This revival came into being between the tenth and twelfth centuries, but its geographical setting was restricted. Only the cities of Chichen Itza and Mayapan witnessed the flowering of this individual art, the product of the fusion of Mayan and Toltec traditions. The newcomers apparently originated from the city of Tula in northern Mexico, and, after lengthy wanderings, the Toltec warriors settled in the northern part of the peninsula and there assimilated the knowledge of their predecessors. The result was an architecture completely different in style from that of the Maya. Tragic in character, grandiose, sometimes sinister and constantly exalting death, it forms a break with the luminous quality of the earlier art.

This modified aesthetic reflects the profound changes to which Mayan thought and religion were subjected after the invasion. The coming of the Itzas corresponded with an extension of the worship of a divinity revered throughout Central America. This was Quetzalcoatal, known as Kukulcan in Yucatan, and the rites in his honor were frequently attended by human sacrifice. Before dealing with these Mexican influences, however, we shall briefly outline the Mayan religion, as far as we can form an idea of it from texts recorded at the time of the Spanish conquest.

Religion and Forms of Worship

The Maya held complex ideas in the spheres of religion and cosmology, reflecting the tribal origins of beliefs emanating from a variety of regions linked by a form of federation. This accounts for the profusion of gods with their frequently contradictory or complementary attributes.

Several characteristic elements should, however, be noted: for instance, a constant feature seems to have been the association of the gods with the four points of the compass. Each divinity was simultaneously unique and fourfold, the four manifestations of the god being associated with the four quarters of the world and four colors. Thus, in the case of the Bacabs, the four divinities supporting the heavens, those representing east, west, north and south were red, black, white and yellow respectively.

Another baffling aspect of this religion lay in the deeply rooted dualism of the gods, each of whom was endowed with a form that was both benevolent and evil. Thus the Chacs or rain gods who were particularly beneficent in the north of the country (where they were worshipped more than anywhere else) were also masters of the storm, and, for this reason, were often portrayed brandishing a symbolic flash of lightning. They can be found on almost every Mayan temple in Yucatan, where the friezes, façades, cornices and angles are punctuated with representations of their stylized masks, long noses and globular eyes. They were four in number and associated with the four points of the compass. This feeling for orientation is of great importance in understanding the planning of Mayan cities.

Itzamna, the god of heaven, who must have been of considerable importance, does not appear so often, but may be found in several different forms. Sometimes he is represented as an old man with a hooked nose, sometimes as a dragon whose image serves as a reflection of the ambiguity of Mayan concepts, for it is provided with a head at each end of its body, one living, the other

The principal divinities of the Mayan pantheon: Itzamna, god of the sky; Chac, the rain god

Yum Kax, the young god of maize; Ah Puch, god of death

The god of human sacrifice; and, last of all, Ixchel, goddess of the moon (after Morley)

dead. The former probably represents the gate of heaven to the east of the world where the heavenly bodies are born, and the latter the western gate where the sun and stars are swallowed up. Itzamna also presided over childbirth and the feminine arts of plaiting and weaving.

The sun god is shown as an ara, a bird which descends to earth to light the sacrificial fires. The goddess of the moon presided over the harvests, but the great divinity of earth and crops was the god of maize. In a civilization based on this life-giving plant, on which prosperity or famine in every case depended, such veneration is easy to understand. The god is portrayed with the features of a beautiful young man endowed with some attributes of the plant. This is a further manifestation of a religion in which the gods are part animal, part vegetable and often part human and part legendary as well. The cult of the young god of maize was so powerful that a few of the rituals of his calendar are still celebrated in present-day Yucatan.

The worship offered to the gods was accompanied by sacrifices and libations: burnt resin, raw or cooked food, the blood of animals or humans. Mayan believers pierced their tongues and the lobes of their ears and offered their own blood as sacrifice. They also, from earliest times, performed human sacrifices by removing the heart, as reliefs at Piedras-Negras and frescoes at Bonampak show. It was not, however, until the Mayan-Toltec period that sacrifices of prisoners of war assumed a scale equal to the horrifying butcheries practised by the Aztecs. The Maya were a more moderate race and, to them, only exceptional occasions warranted the practice of human sacrifice.

On the other hand, periodic sacrifices to the rain god seem to have been carried out at an early period in Chichen Itza, the victims being thrown alive into the sacred well where they perished by drowning.

The subterranean world, ruled over by the nine lords of the night, was also accorded its sacrifices which were linked with funerary rites. In the southern province chieftains were buried in pomp, as we know from discoveries made in the crypt at Palenque. A priest-king was entombed in the heart of a vast pyramid and six of his intimates were sacrificed at his side, probably either to accompany and serve him in the other world, or to gain the favor of the divinities of

Human sacrifice by heart excision, as shown in a painting from the Temple of the Warriors at Chichen Itza (after Morley)

the underworld on his behalf. On the other hand, in Yucatan, during the Mayan period, the nobles were cremated; one more example of the profound cultural difference between the two regions of Mayan territory.

Notwithstanding the complexity of the Mayan religion, many aspects of which remain totally unexplained to us, the faith which animated them must have been intense. The number of temples, pyramids and altars surviving in their country bear witness to the deeply religious aspect of every activity carried out in their jungle cities.

The Indian Character

Although the Maya were sufficiently devoted to their religion to expend the greater part of their energies on building temples, this was not their only characteristic worthy of mention. All their qualities were remarkable and were, to a large extent, responsible for the success of the civilization which they evolved. The Maya were intensely calm, disciplined and peace-loving, seldom indulging in war. Even today there are comparatively few murderers to be found in Yucatan. This innate pacifism is understandable when we recall their constant struggle against nature. This daily battle served to canalize their natural desire for combat, for few peoples have succeeded in forcing themselves on such a hostile territory, where survival is ceaselessly threatened by the devastating vegetation.

Decency and honesty, together with a strongly developed social sense, which manifested itself in collective effort and teamwork, completed their characteristics. One need spend only a short time in Yucatan to notice how gentle and courteous the Indians are and how little given to excess, except in regard to alcohol, introduced to them by Europeans. They are not afflicted by either the spirit of violence or of competition. The latter characteristic probably vanished as

the result of foreign infiltration, possibly following on the decline of the period of high civilization. For the immense achievements of the past could not have come about without a sense of ambition and a will directed particularly towards co-ordinated effort so that each new creation might surpass the previous one.

Life and Death of a Civilization

On the peninsula separating the isthmus of Tehuantepec from that of Salvador and Honduras, an individual civilization sprang into brief but intense life. Between the period when the Germanic tribes, who were to overturn the ascendancy of Rome, overran Northern Europe and the end of Arab expansion, the Maya erected numerous splendid cities. When the West was a victim of convulsions caused by displaced peoples, Central America achieved stability and produced the most glorious of pre-Columbian civilizations.

Six or seven centuries of high intellectual and artistic prosperity enabled a culture provided with the chief inventions of humanity to arise out of practically nothing. Six or seven centuries permitted a small nation split up into tribes, scattered throughout virgin forest, to scale fleetingly the heights of a great civilization. This is an almost greater mystery than the irremediable, absolute decline which put an end to this brilliant destiny.

What is meant by the individual lives of civilizations? Are their destinies really similar to those of human beings, consisting of birth, development and death? Why is a flashing start, followed by a brilliant apotheosis, likewise condemned to an absolute full stop? Such questions assail us when we are confronted with such a strange culture. For, though the Mayan world developed during the period when the great civilizations of Teotihuacan, Monte Alban and Xochicalco also came into being, unlike them it did not leave behind it a heritage from which newcomers would benefit. In Mayan territory, there were no heirs to the priests who were driven from the jungle temples. Only a silent covering of vegetation fell over the forgotten cities.

In the West there are many dead civilizations, but almost always there is a military or economic explanation for their decadence or annihilation. Neither Tikal nor Copan, by contrast, ever seems to have suffered invasion. Palenque and Uxmal died out because the life force of the civilization which had brought them into being expired. Countless explanations have been called on to solve the riddle.

One fact remains: it is rare for an ancient culture of seven centuries to disappear without bequeathing its successors some share of its learning and knowledge. This unique fate, solitary death and total abandonment, confers a dramatic aspect on the Mayan world.

Excess of Hypothetical Knowledge

At the conclusion of this brief survey of the background of Mayan architecture, we may say that their civilization is often paradoxical. Though neolithic on more than one count, it had knowledge of writing. This writing, however, teaches us almost nothing concerning social, political, economic and religious organization. Every stele and every codex illuminates one preoccupation only: religious chronology and ritual designed to celebrate an exact date. Even if we were able in a very short space of time to read all the texts at our disposal and also had in our possession previously destroyed texts, it seems we would make few discoveries apart from mathematical calculations referring to the cycles of the planets, eclipses and the tropical year.

The world of the Maya will not rise from the shades of prehistory through our understanding of their texts, and for this reason we must turn to the archaeologists for help in elucidation. Buildings are the best witnesses of human behaviour in this part of the world where all other traces are swept away by the ever-present humidity. Architecture will give us an understanding of many aspects of Mayan life that have disappeared: social and hierarchical systems, the position of the family, religious and funerary ceremonies. It can even provide us with valuable information on the organization of work within the community.

Nevertheless, the results gained from an architectural examination must remain hypothetical. Conclusions can be based only on probabilities and not on scientific certainties. On many counts it is the destiny of Mayan civilization to remain mysterious.

Unfortunately, the four or five most notable specialists have sometimes expressed diametrically opposed ideas. It is necessary, therefore, in this book to make a personal evaluation of Mayan architecture, while recognizing that, with the relative speed at which our knowledge of the Mayan civilization is changing, any concept is subject to re-evaluation in the light of new information.

Plates

Uxmal (Yucatan)

67 **Palace of the Governor.** This building, like most Puuc architecture at Uxmal, dates from the eighth-ninth centuries. It is 322 feet long, 39 feet in depth and 28 feet high. The façade is divided by a horizontal binder over 13 doors leading to 20 vaulted chambers. The stone mosaic frieze is made up of 20,000 blocks of sculptured limestone.

68 The central block, with the throne of the two-headed jaguar in the foreground. The façade, with the bare wall at the base, is typical of the Puuc style. The symmetrical, yet cleverly irregular, arrangement of the doors indicates a lively feeling for composition.

70 Two corners decorated with the traditional marks of Chac, the rain god. They are strictly stylized and repeated five times one above the other.

71 Interior of the great chamber in the middle of the central block. Sixty-five feet long and less than 16 feet wide, it is covered by a typical lofty Mayan vault and lit by three doors. A single opening (left) leads into the very dark rear chamber.

72 The link between the central block and the wings is formed by lofty vaults. The arches were originally left wide open, but later were walled up and fronted with columns.

73 The central entrance doorway, surmounted by a great decorative feature which forms the hub of the frieze design. The horizontal elements represent celestial dragons one above the other.

74 The frieze consists of wide Greek key-ornaments set over a network resembling an openwork grating.

75 Detail of the substructure emphasized by a powerful molding with a regular rhythm.

76 **House of the Tortoises.** Lateral façade. A range of engaged balusters is compressed between two moldings.

77 The building takes its name from the tortoises carved in relief on the upper cornice.

78 **Pyramid of the Magician.** The great east staircase leading to the upper temple. A modern entrance gives access to an earlier temple buried in the masonry.

79 The western staircase bordered by masks of Chac.

80 **The Quadrilateral of the Nunnery** from the Governor's Palace. Right: the Pyramid of the Magician.

82 The Quadrilateral from the top of the Pyramid of the Magician.

83 West building of the Quadrilateral from the porticoed gallery at the foot of the northern palace.

84 Façade of the north palace of the Nunnery: a great plumed serpent completely surrounds the mosaic decoration.

85 Detail of the head and tail of the plumed serpent. A human face may be seen in the monster's open mouth. Here the sculpture turns to high relief.

86 Lower gallery of the north building: its square pillars support a frieze of highly stylized Chac masks.

87 This axial view of the gallery shows the fine vaulted ceiling crossed by wooden stays at two levels. The doors on the right lead to the rear chambers.

88 On the façade of the western palace of the Nunnery, this detached figure of a guardian, armed with a cudgel, is a rare example of Puuc statuary.

89 Frieze of the western palace of the Nunnery. A faithful representation of a pisé hut with roof of thatch and square door. These symbolic huts, resembling those inhabited by the majority of the Maya, surmount the entrances to each of the palace chambers and clearly explain the function of dwelling place assigned to these stone buildings. The grille in the background, from which the decoration stands out, is formed of rows of St Andrew's crosses.

90 Decorative motif over the central door of the western palace of the Nunnery. In the center a statue is protected by a kind of canopy.

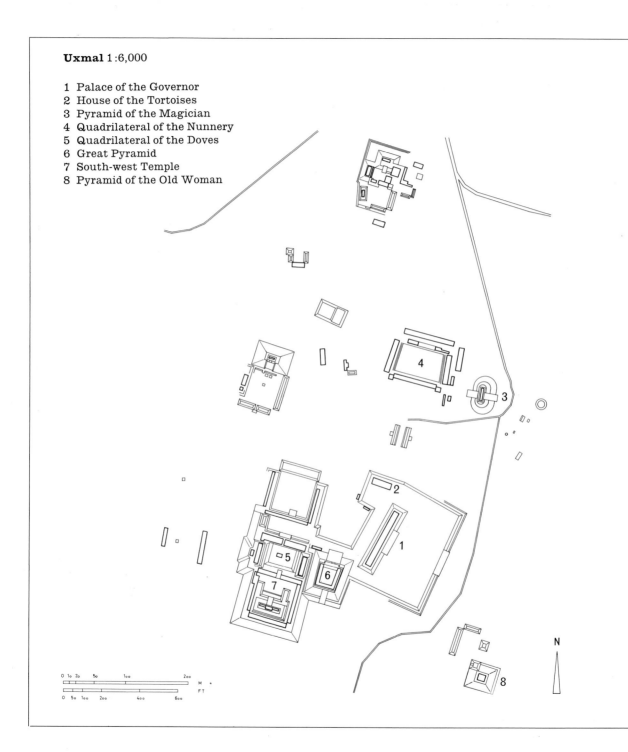

Uxmal 1:6,000

1 Palace of the Governor
2 House of the Tortoises
3 Pyramid of the Magician
4 Quadrilateral of the Nunnery
5 Quadrilateral of the Doves
6 Great Pyramid
7 South-west Temple
8 Pyramid of the Old Woman

0 1o 2o 5o   1oo   2oo   M
0 5o 1oo   2oo   4oo   6oo   FT

N

Palace of the Governor, Uxmal: elevation and plan 1:750

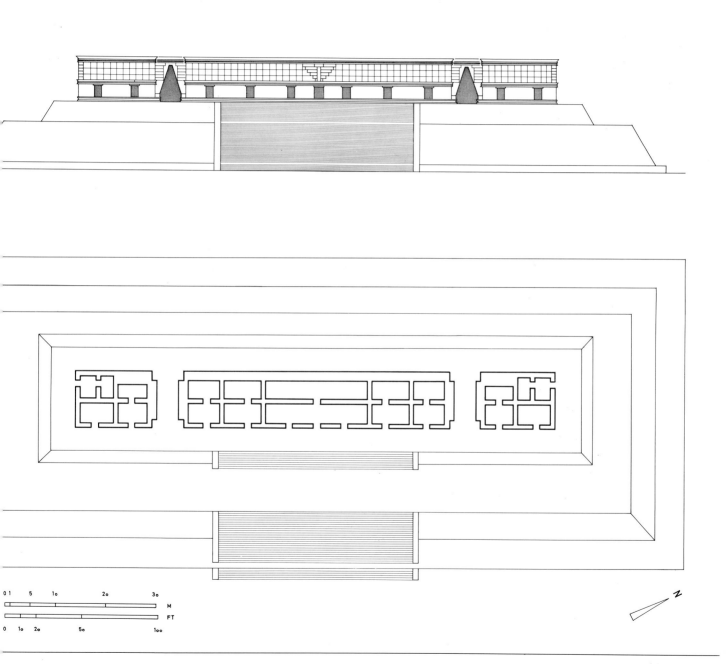

0 1   5   1o   2o   3o
M

FT
0   1o   2o   5o   1oo

N

Notes

Uxmal and Yucatan

The vegetation of the northern district of Yucatan is far from having the destructive power of the tall forest trees of the Peten. The high foliage with its damp undergrowth is here replaced by dry, deciduous scrub, and trees seldom grow higher than forty feet. Moreover, the rains are less frequent and less heavy and, for this reason, destruction by natural forces assumes less importance in this zone.

Thus, the archaeological sites of the Puuc style, particularly at Uxmal, are in a state where reconstruction is much easier than at Tikal or Palenque. In many cases, the chief damage consists of the collapse of the wooden lintels surmounting the wide palace doors. The fall of these decayed ties has usually been accompanied by the crumbling of a whole section of the stone mosaic frieze. Puuc decorative motifs are, for the most part, regular and endlessly repetitive, like those of a carpet. Provided, therefore, a sufficiently large part of the ornament remains intact, it is possible to set about reconstruction, with the help of the pieces of the puzzle scattered over the ground.

If we consult the photographic evidence published by Frederico Mariscal in 1928 at the start of the excavations carried out at Uxmal by the Mexican Ministry of Education, we realize that this site, visited by Waldeck and Stephens a little less than a century previously, possessed sufficient grandeur to stimulate the idea of possible reconstruction.

The conservation work boldly undertaken by the Mexicans just after the Revolution resulted in the preservation of these architectural treasures. It is chiefly because of the restorations carried out after 1938 that the principal buildings of Uxmal have regained an incomparable splendor. These large-scale works were supervised by the archaeologist José Erosa Peniche of the Instituto Nacional de Antropologia e Historia, and today the tourist is able to see an extraordinarily imposing group of monuments, almost intact.

Nevertheless, there are still several buildings which await restoration. These include the Quadrilateral of the Doves, the Great Pyramid, the Pyramid of the Old Woman, the South Temple, the West Quadrilateral and the Ball-Court. The chief buildings, however, especially the Palace of the Governor and the Quadrilateral of the Nunnery, have regained their former splendor.

Superimpositions

As with all Mayan buildings, those at Uxmal were not completed straight away and underwent many changes. The number of buildings superimposed is sometimes amazing: the Pyramid of the Magician consists of five temples enclosed within one another like a nest of tables, probably spanning close on three centuries.

The first, on ground level, can be seen beneath the great west staircase; the second was discovered below the last staircase, in which an opening has recently been arranged to give access to it. Temple III was reached by a staircase on the east side which was, in its turn, buried under some later steps. In front of it, forming a narthex, is Temple IV in the Chenes style, its façade representing the mask of the god Chac whose jaws serve as the door. Finally, Temple V has caused the pyramid to be considerably raised, as the roof-comb of Temple III is preserved beneath its floor. There is one extremely odd feature of these transformations by successive superimpositions: the temples changed their orientations. Possibly these architectural modifications involved alterations in the religious role of the building or in the form of worship.

Another strange superimposition concerns the two arches linking the wings of the Palace of the Governor to the central block. These great vaults were originally open the whole width of the building, but were then closed by a wall to half their height and fronted by a pair of columns in the form of a portico supporting a peculiar covering shaped like a hut whose roof imitated the thatch and palm leaves of the traditional pisé constructions. All that is now left of these additions is a section of the shafts of the columns: these supported wooden lintels which have rotted away and caused the collapse of all the roofing subsequently added in front of the arches.

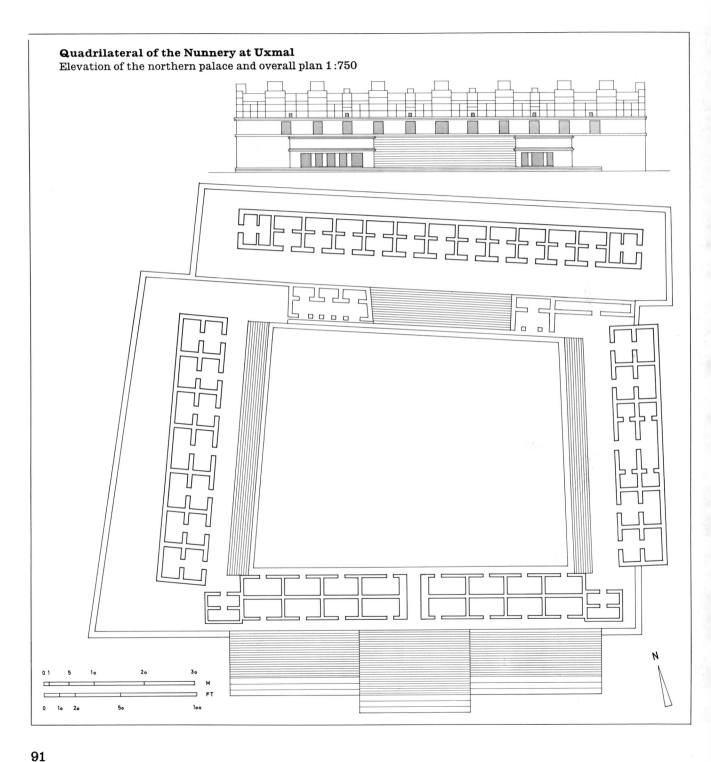

Quadrilateral of the Nunnery at Uxmal
Elevation of the northern palace and overall plan 1:750

0 1 5 1o 2o 3o M
0 1o 2o 5o 1oo FT

N

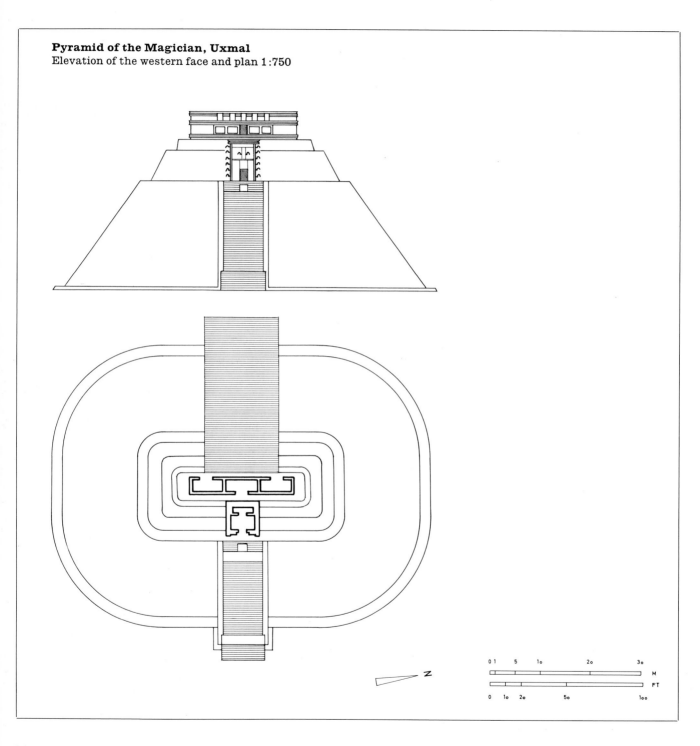

Pyramid of the Magician, Uxmal
Elevation of the western face and plan 1:750

0 1   5   1o   2o   3o M

0   1o 2o   5o   1oo FT

N

92

2. Forms and Functions of Buildings

The countless Mayan cities scattered over the peninsula of Yucatan, Guatemala and Western Honduras provide an unbelievably rich and varied store of architecture of incontestable beauty. It is essential to remember that only the heritage of stone has survived: all buildings fashioned of wood, pisé or thatch have been lost for ever. The vast majority of the Maya lived in huts covered with palm leaves. Although these have disappeared, it does not mean that nothing is known about the homes of these people or that the huts contemporary with the great pre-Columbian buildings have left no traces for archaeologists.

The huts: an unchanging architecture

Traces of the foundations of these primitive huts are still sometimes visible on the ground. Holes for posts, too, provide us with a key to their proportions, and the sculptured friezes of the palaces often present them down to the last detail. Drawings in the codices, paintings and graffiti also contribute to our sure knowledge.

One basic fact emerges from this evidence: the chozas, as these huts are called in Spanish, have not altered in the space of 2,000 years and most of the huts of present-day Yucatan may be regarded as authentic Mayan buildings. This is of basic importance in the understanding of all Mayan architecture, for it allows us to grasp the close connection between buildings made of perishable materials and their successors transposed into stone and mortar.

Indeed, if there is any art whose origins can be traced back through form, function and decorative elements despite the substitutions of one basic material for another, it is that of Mayan architecture. Everywhere there are signs of a genuine transposition into stone after the modifications made necessary by the properties of the new material. The fundamental characteristics remain, however, as immutable as the peasant huts themselves. There are two or three of these characteristics which we must describe as they condition the structure of all Mayan buildings.

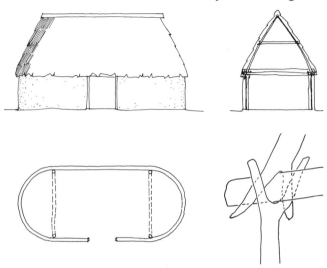

Mayan hut: elevation, plan, section and detail of the construction of the framework with the aid of forked branches

The huts are almost always set on platforms reached by means of small staircases. These pedestals of dried earth and stone are seldom more than two feet high and often less. The most ancient huts, traces of which have been found by archaeologists at Uaxactun, were also built on these low platforms, whose sole function was to save the houses from being flooded during the heavy tropical rains. The dwelling which stood on this foundation of beaten earth, was rectangular or oval in plan—and measured roughly 16 by 10 feet. A single square door pierced one of the longer sides. Usually there was no other opening in the walls or the roof, nor was there a window or a chimney.

The walls were made of plaited branches and kept in position by large vertical posts; they formed a protective shell to which could be applied a facing of pisé often whitened with lime. In the case of recent examples, the walls are sometimes made of masonry, but wood is always used for the framework of the roof.

The roof was supported by tree trunks kept in position by means of a fork at one end. A covering of thatch and palm leaves was placed over the lofty rafters set at an angle of more than 60°. The ridge of the roof was as long as the front of the hut and at the two ends—if the sides were curved—the covering formed a half cone so that the roof encircled the hut.

The height of the interior exceeded its ground measurements; the space extended between the two parallel sets of walls and then, in the absence of ceiling or upper floor, formed a great inverted "V" beneath the roof.

There was no form of chimney to carry away smoke because the Maya did not cook in their huts, but outside beneath a lean-to which sheltered them from wind and rain.

The method of covering, the lack of openings and the height of the interiors all combined to keep the huts cool. This system of insulation based on a thick roofing of vegetable material may be found in almost all tropical countries.

The standard proportions, the form of the interior space, the door placed on the long side and the relative darkness of these huts of wood and thatch are repeated in most of the stone buildings, both palaces and temples. By a paradox, pre-Columbian interiors are typified by their mean, cramped appearance when compared with the majestic grandeur of their façades and massive exteriors. The Maya were unable to free themselves from the pattern of the huts and one of the major characteristics of their architecture stems from an exaggerated conservatism whose influence we shall find in all forms of representation used by the Maya.

The Platforms

Transpositon into stone was only realized in successive stages. The discoveries of archaeologists, particularly those at Uaxactun, show that the first Mayan temples were fashioned of perishable materials similar to those used in the huts. For a long period the shrines were constructed entirely of wood and thatch. The supporting platforms, on the other hand, reached a state of perfection much earlier, and were increased in height and proportion. Coverings of cement and stucco were substituted for dry stone enclosing a core of beaten earth, and lofty staircases led to the summits of these rough pyramids.

Here again conservatism was at work; for the pyramidal form undoubtedly stemmed from the early use of earth piled up in accordance with its natural tendency to form a slope. The use of this form continued even when the builders later adopted more resistant and solid material which would have made possible the construction of vertical platforms.

As their importance increased, these platforms, which were originally strictly utilitarian, eventually became essential architectural characteristics. At Tikal the pyramids, exclusive of the actual temples, were as much as 130 feet high, a long way from the early attempts at Uaxactun where the famous stucco pyramid, ornamented with gigantic masks and flanked by four staircases, was no more than 26 feet off the ground. Yet this building, discovered by Ricketson, forms the first link in a chain of amazing developments. This pyramid E VII (building VII of group E) dates from the second century B.C.

The progressive raising of the platform necessitated the transformation of the small staircases which at first consisted of no more than three or four steps. Their flights became steeper, the handling of the tiers bolder and more abrupt: thus they grew into a dominating factor, and, undoubtedly formed, along with the pyramids, one of the constant elements of pre-Columbian civilization.

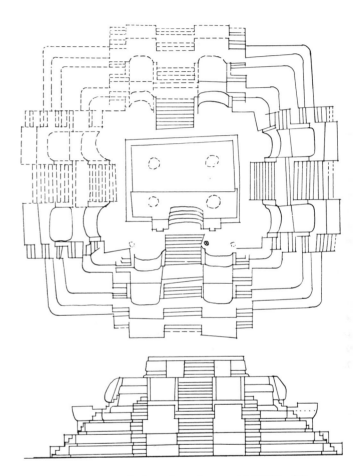

Uaxactun: plan and elevation of pyramid E VII with stucco decoration (after Marquina)

The Mayan Vault

Transposition into stone did not stop with the pedestals of the buildings. After having for a long time resembled the simple huts of wood and thatch, the temples were given walls of stone

95

and masonry. This advance was, however, temporarily halted at roof level. Then, no later than the beginning of the fourth century, came the crowning achievement of Mayan architecture: the great invention of a masonry vault.

Here again the solution adopted stems from a strict sense of tradition. A completely novel type of vault appears, based on the interior arrangement of the huts. There is a change of material, but the essentials of the interior of the chozas remain basically unaltered.

Technically the Mayan vault can only be explained by the transposition into stone of a pre-existing form, for it certainly does not derive from ideas compatible with the material in hand. Moreover, this lack of adaptation explains the absence of subsequent evolution. The Mayan vault is not a genuine type of vault, defined as a system of thrusts counterbalanced by stones whose joins are arranged in a radial pattern with a keystone at the top of the curve; nor is it a corbeled vault whose horizontal courses act only as vertical supports and whose corbel stones are merely held by the weight of the material. The Mayan vault has often been described as a corbel vault because of the discovery in the early buildings of the Peten and Yucatan of examples constructed with fairly wide, overhanging blocks which allow a single stone to close the space defined by the two retaining walls. It is clear, however, that, without the use of cement, such a vault would certainly have collapsed.

Without mortar and fillings of rubble the Mayan vault would not be possible, and the best proof of the non-functional character of these slabs is that they were soon exchanged for an ordinary facing.

In its commonest and simplest form this type of vault rests on two walls which thicken as they rise until they unite to form an enclosed space.

a)

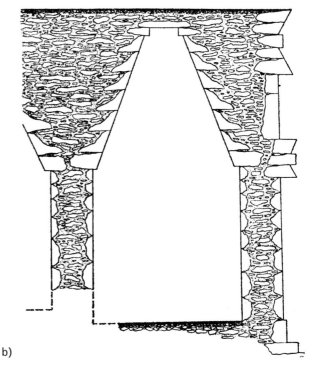

b)

Mayan vaults: (a) Archaic type, constructed with the aid of slabs (b) Classic type with stone facing and concrete masonry (after Andrews)

Possibly this may not have been so in the earliest examples, where it would seem that the Maya inclined the walls towards the interior above a certain height, so that the two planes joined at the summit of the building. Thus a twofold transformation took place: the walls became thinner with the passing of the centuries, and the angle of the roof, when seen from outside, became progressively straighter.

The early stages of this development produced a form of mansard roof. A band above the vertical wall inclined slightly inwards and was surmounted by the two-sided but almost flat roof. The band soon became ornamented with stone or stucco as at Palenque and thus turned into a frieze. It was this decoration which probably caused the frieze to be reset vertically, so that it not only became easier to distinguish the motifs but they were better protected from the tropical rains.

Henceforward the roof flattened out completely and the exterior of the building took on the appearance of a cube, except when, as in some of the late Mayan constructions at Tulum, there was an overhang.

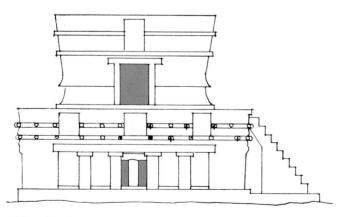

Temple of the Frescoes at Tulum: the walls of the building clearly widen towards the summit (after Marquina)

The most surprising feature, however, is the traditionalism which led the Maya to perpetuate the interior design of all their buildings, when, once they had at their disposal a sufficiently hard and resistant form of mortar, they could have freed themselves from the formal limits of the past. Without knowing it, they possessed the means which enabled the Romans to create the most imaginative interiors known in history. Why the Maya were not also able to do so is a mystery historians have not been able to solve.

Types of Buildings

The following is the basic vocabulary which enabled the Maya to produce the greatest profusion of buildings and cities in the heart of the tropical forest: a slope or platform, walls fashioned of masonry, and a type of block roofing whose design owes nothing to the properties of the material employed. In short it was a purely static architectural system, ignorant of the pressures exerted by arches, vaults, or domes as we know them; it never learnt the language of dynamics which would have permitted the expansion of wide interior spaces.

The paradox of Mayan interior space lies in the fact that it is always weaker than the material mass enveloping it. The buildings resemble hollow monoliths, far removed from the delicate shells and vast interior spaces produced by the Romans.

The Maya built their monuments with the help of architectural elements that combined technical knowledge, of which the discovery of concrete was the most startling, with the embryo mechanics of tensions and thrusts. From this it followed logically that the range of their buildings was limited. Their restricted formal vocabulary, coupled with their inability to provide roofs in excess of a given capacity, condemned their architecture to an undoubted monotony in the interplay of function and design. These restrictions were, however, to a great extent counterbalanced by a feeling for grandiose town-planning which added beauty to the exteriors.

The Pyramid

The term 'pyramid' in its purely geometrical sense can only be applied to the great constructions of the Egyptians, whose bases are in fact polygonal and whose faces are defined by triangular planes meeting at the summit. Nevertheless, the Mayan buildings with rectangular or square bases are really truncated pyramids and those of more complex design with oval bases are related to truncated cones.

The function of these constructions differs as much as their design. Sometimes they are artificial hills supporting temples, at others they are tombs; sometimes they fulfil both functions. Two essentially different types must, however, be distinguished: some pyramids represent a culminating point and are sacred; no one may set foot on them. Others are meant to be climbed; the priests ascend them to meet the gods.

The Central American peoples, like the Assyrians, crowned their pyramidal constructions with lofty temples. The pyramid was no more than a monumental pedestal, and established a vertical movement between the world below and that of the gods.

There are cases where the Mayan pyramids may have served as tombs. The most amazing example of this type of usage has already been mentioned—the famous crypt discovered in the heart of the Pyramid of Inscriptions at Palenque by Alberto Ruz in 1952.

It is a curious fact that, after their initial gropings, all civilizations at the start of their development, seem to go through a period when their architecture assumes a gigantic scale. Just as the great pyramids of Dashur and Gizeh are some of the oldest in Egypt, so at Tikal, the ancient capital of the Peten, the loftiest buildings are to be found. The platforms alone are 115 and 130 feet high and the roof line of the temples as much as 200 or 230 feet above the ground. Mayan sanctuaries of later dates never attained such heights.

Steps and Staircases

The Mayan pyramids, like those at Djoser in Egypt and the ziggurats of Mesopotamia, are made up of several vertical or inclined steps which break the sloping faces. At Tikal the steps have a complex outline which succeeds in giving the building an impression of lightness. The angle of the slope exceeds 45° and is sometimes as much as 60°. Thus the ascending staircases have steps which are higher than they are wide.

The first temples with pyramidal bases sometimes have staircases on all four sides as at Uaxactun in the Peten and Acanceh in Yucatan, but, starting with the pyramids of Tikal, steps leading to the upper platform are often found only on the forward side. At Uxmal, however, two staircases mount opposite sides of the Pyramid of the Magician, giving access to two different temples. Finally, at the magnificent Castillo of Chichen Itza, Mayan-Toltec architecture rediscovered the formula of four staircases.

Some ramps are embedded in the mass of the pyramid, others project clearly from the face, giving the impression of an independent, linked element. The slope of the staircase is often more reduced than that of the building and, in these cases, it makes a powerful projection at the base of the pyramid, uniting with it at the level of the upper platform. The stairs usually stop abruptly at the edges of the steps but are sometimes bounded by strips, either plain as at Palenque or decorated as on the Hieroglyphic Stairways at Copan. None of them, however, has proper hand-rails or balustrades.

The Upper Temple

The temple itself stands on the quadrangular platform at the top of the pyramid. Here, and especially at Tikal, we again come across the constituent elements of the primitive huts. First there is the low pedestal reached by a few steps set on the axis of the monumental staircase, then the vertical walls pierced by the traditional square doorway on the forward side of the building and, finally, the steeply inclined roof.

The sanctuary is, however, surmounted by a new element: a lofty crest of stone, sometimes ornamented with perforations or motifs in relief, which rises well above the roof. This is the roof-comb; its function appears to be purely decorative, but it is none the less typical of early Mayan architecture. It, too, probably derives from the transposition into stone of some wooden structure designed to distinguish the most important houses from the ordinary peasant huts.

Once past the threshold, the temple surprises us by the small dimensions of its interior. Though the façades of the temples surmounting the pyramids of Tikal range from 33 to 90 feet in length, the rooms within measure no more than between 15 and 23 feet. In the huge Temple V, for example, the façade measures 80 feet but the shrine no more than 16 feet, only one-fifth of the building.

These tiny rooms are identical in design and proportion to the interiors of the huts. To enlarge the interior space without, however, abandoning the basic unit of the primitive hut, the Maya conceived the idea of duplicating or even triplicating the rooms, placing them in enfilade in a succession of oblongs, communicating with one another by means of square doorways similar to the opening giving access to the building. The result was the equivalent of two or three adjacent huts situated behind one another, at right angles to the axis of the entrance.

This solution is constantly to be found in Mayan architecture, and the rooms, communicating on their wider sides, offer the most varied combinations.

In the early buildings the interiors are so reduced in scale as to be almost ridiculous. In Temple II at Tikal, for instance, though it has three rooms instead of two as at Temple III or one as at Temple V, the volume of masonry surrounding the rooms amounts to three times that of the interior spaces. Thus in the case of a temple occupying an area 860 square feet, the rooms take up little more than 200 square feet. The relationship of the volumes is even more revealing, especially if calculated in conjunction with the actual pyramid when the interior space works out as being no more than a one hundred and fiftieth part of the whole construction.

Such proportions were characteristic of the formative period. Mayan buildings never achieved a really practical balance of mass and interior space: the volume of walls and roof almost always exceeded that of the rooms. There were, however, numerous attempts at improving the position. Already, at Palenque, the walls of the Temple of the Sun were incomparably thinner than those at Tikal. Simultaneously an ingenious solution was adopted to replace the inner communicating doors with less strongly defined subdivisions. It was discovered that, by combining the two oblong spaces, each of which resembled the design of the traditional hut, with a third identical space set in the axis of the entrance at right angles to the other two with which it formed a link, there resulted a form of vaulted, double transept. This novel formula brought about an improved spatial continuity, yet did not meet with the success that might

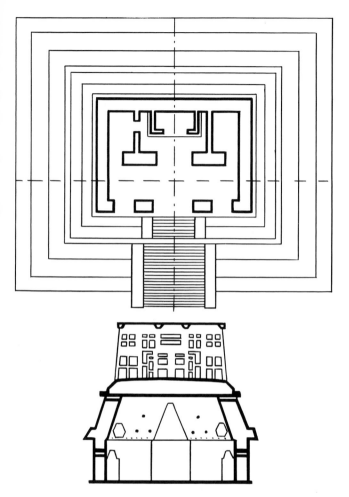

Temple of the Sun at Palenque: plan and section
(after Marquina)

have been expected of it. The city of Palenque seems to have been the only place where it was practised on a vast scale.

Experts do not agree on the functions allotted to the majority of Mayan buildings, but it is clear that the pyramids were crowned with temples about whose religious significance there can be no doubt. The far end of the room is often taken up with a kind of platform or roofed dais resembling a tabernacle of impressive propor-

tions, and the wall behind it is covered with representations of gods to whom priests pay sacrificial homage.

Palaces with Chambers

Although there can be no doubts regarding the function of the temples, the same cannot be said of the huge constructions which the first Spanish conquerors called palaces.

In contrast to the pyramids, where the stresses are vertical, the palaces are distinguished by their widespread horizontal lines. Both forms of building, however, derive from the same elements; the temples are set on pyramidal platforms, and the palaces also are built on level expanses of ground reached by staircases. Finally, the ranges of chambers in the palaces are still based on the interiors of the primitive huts and their arrangement is similar: behind each of the many doorways pierced in the façades, there is still the single chamber typical of the hut, set at right angles to the entrance. When the palace consists of two or more chambers in depth, they communicate with one another by means of doors set in the longer walls or, very occasionally, in the shorter ones.

However, the size of the palaces and the large number of chambers they contain allows for an infinite variety of interior divisions and a wide range of plans. Some palaces consist merely of a single range of chambers placed side by side parallel to the façade; they do not communicate with one another and their doors all give on to the same front. Usually, however, the chambers are set in two rows in which case there are two possible forms of arrangement. Sometimes the openings are on one front only; the rear chambers do not communicate directly with the exterior, but have doors leading to the outer ones. Sometimes the building has a central, spinal wall and the chambers are set on either side of this: in this case, they do not communicate with one another but have doors opening on to two sides of the palace. There are particularly good examples of this latter arrangement at Nakum and in the south wing of the Nunnery at Uxmal.

Sometimes the building may consist of three or four chambers, one behind the other, some of which are linked to the exterior only by means of right angled corridors; or all the openings may be on the same axis so that it is possible to cross the entire building. Examples of this arrangement are comparatively rare, however.

As a general rule, the chambers are all the same size. Sometimes, as at the Palace of the Governor at Uxmal, the central chambers are larger. Some measure 65 feet by 11.5 feet but the usual length is 20 to 26 feet and the width never more than 15 feet, proportions which are typical of the huts.

Some palaces are of several storeys, involving alternative methods of construction. The chambers may simply be built one above the other as at Tikal where there is a succession of three storeys, or they may form a series of levels in recession as at Sayil and Edzna. In the latter case the shape of the building is almost pyramidal.

There are, therefore, numerous possibilities and combinations, and here the Maya used their imagination to the best advantage. Despite the small scale of their basic unit, they succeeded in constructing gigantic buildings up to 300 feet in length. At Nakum one palace consists of no fewer than 48 chambers, while the Nunnery at Uxmal has a total of 80 in its four buildings and resembles a vast cloister with numerous individual cells. It was because of this likeness that the Spanish conquerors gave the name of nunneries to the great palaces of Uxmal and Chichen Itza.

Corridor palaces

The palaces formed of ranges of chambers under the same roof but without inter-communication should not be confused with a type of corridor palace similar to those at Palenque. Their function must have been very different, as their plan shows. Instead of being occupied by a string of small chambers scarcely any of which had communicating doors, these corridor palaces result from the suppression of the side walls separating the rooms. This original form of design probably sprang from special requirements and is seen to best advantage at Palenque and in the region of the Usumacinta. There are few examples of it outside these localities.

Instead of being composed of façades pierced by doors beyond which are the chamber ranges, these palaces appear to present two colonnades wide open to the exterior, on either side of a central wall. Indeed, the apertures are so close to one another that the wall of the façade is reduced to a series of supporting pillars or galleries covered with the traditional Mayan vault.

These long covered passages apparently form the elements of a ceremonial center whose function is clearly distinct from that of the other palaces.

The Question of Habitability

The problem of the function of the chambered palaces is a question which has aroused widely opposing theories. There are many expert archaeologists who think that these vast architectural complexes were centers of religion, occupied only at intervals. These arguments cannot be ignored especially if they are advanced by experts of the caliber of Thompson and Krickeberg, and, for this reason, we append some of the views outlined by the former in his "Rise and Fall of Mayan Civilisation".

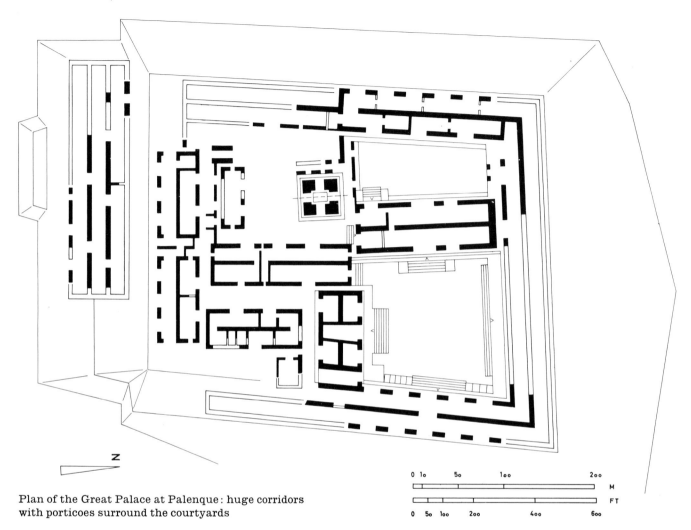

Plan of the Great Palace at Palenque: huge corridors
with porticoes surround the courtyards

In his opinion, the Mayan cities were ceremonial centers, not planned towns. The stone
buildings were not suitable for permanent
habitation; they had no fireplaces or windows,
though some rooms had air vents in the walls.
They were also damp and badly lit. The inner
rooms relied entirely on the light which filtered
through the door of the vestibule and were
almost dark. They could not have been lived in,
nor was it possible to cook inside. Thompson's
theory was that these buildings were occupied by

novices and, perhaps, by civil dignitaries during
long periods of abstinence preceding the chief
festivals. The uncomfortable conditions would
have been exactly what they sought.

His views, Thompson avers, are confirmed by
the practices of some Mayan communities in the
highlands of Guatemala who gather indoors to
perform prescribed ceremonies. In our opinion,
however, it is difficult to reconcile the type of

building designed for communal reunions with the palaces and their individual chambers, which are more like cells than assembly halls. Moreover, it would be interesting to know to what extent the natives today are influenced by Christian usages; for the idea of a church as a place of reunion had no equivalent in the Mayan world.

There is, however, an attraction in a thesis which favors an exclusively religious function for these stone buildings; for it is well known that in the majority of the great antique civilizations, stone constructions were reserved for the gods and the ceremonial of the priests, whilst the common people and the nobility lived in houses of clay.

Even though they bring us back to the idea of transposition into stone, which has hitherto been considered as being of basic importance, it must be confessed that Thompson's arguments are not wholly convincing. When he speaks of the absence of fireplaces it does not prove much: for we have seen that the Maya never cooked in their huts, but in the open under a lean-to. Neither is the absence of windows decisive, for the huts did not possess any. Nor could the inconvenience of damp have been as great as Thompson thought: as long as the roofs were carefully maintained, there was nothing to fear from the infiltration of rain water.

On the other hand, the cool atmosphere of the relatively high rooms, sealed off by the vast thickness of the masonry, must have been a decided asset in the often sweltering latitudes of the Maya. The absence of windows can undoubtedly be explained in the same way.

In short, to suppose that the Mayan palaces were uninhabitable because they lacked windows and fireplaces is similar to considering Versailles a religious building merely because it has no bathrooms or lavatories. We must guard against drawing conclusions based on our own habits and taste.

Thus it can be asserted that the Mayan palaces were no less comfortable than their thatched huts and there are strong grounds for supposing that these vast buildings were inhabited. Moreover, it is difficult to see why religious edifices, destined for intermittent occupation in accordance with strictly determined precepts, should have required such a variety of arrangement and plan. Such unbounded richness of combinations can be explained only by the need to make adaptations to varying necessities of life.

It is an acceptable theory that Mayan dignitaries lived in these immense palaces, surrounded by crowds of servants and devoting their entire time to the government of the city, religious obligations, astronomical calculations and architectural plans. Such a specialized élite would appear perfectly compatible with the ideas of order, discipline and exactitude regulating the social hierarchy of the Maya.

Pyramid-palaces and palace-pyramids

Our detailed sketch of architectural development is, in fact, far too schematic. There are many exceptions, aberrations of design, and throwbacks to archaic methods, right up to the final decades of Mayan civilization. Moreover, the strict division made for convenience between temples and palaces is not always so well defined. There are bastard examples and intermediate types, both of some importance. We have already implied this in referring to palaces with storeys in recession. There are several examples of pyramid-palaces or palace-pyramids of this design, which seem to combine the functions of both types of building, in accordance with a formula that is both harmonious and original. Buildings of this kind are rare, but may be found at Yaxchilan, Edzna and elsewhere.

The most spectacular is probably that at Edzna, a five-storey palace on a 200 feet square base. The structure is over 65 feet high and forms a step pyramid, each of whose stages bears a series of chambers, the majority of which are set in double ranges. A monumental staircase leading to the upper temple mounts the front of the pyramid. This temple consists of three rooms, one of which opens on to the side away from the entrance, and is topped with a high roof-comb.

This complex building clearly defies our previous classifications. According to the Mexican archaeologist, Alberto Ruz, it is a primitive pyramid to which a succession of vaulted chambers has been added. After the first alteration the stages bore one range of rooms each, and these were eventually doubled on the two lower levels.

The strongest of these intermediate designs are those in the Rio Bec style. The Rio Bec region lies to the north of the Peten and forms the setting for a very individual type of building. One of the great monuments at Xpuhil, for instance, though in a very ruinous state, offers the undeniable characteristics of a palace with twelve chambers. At each end of the eastern façade and in the center of the west front, however, are curious towers of solid masonry exactly reproducing the appearance of three pyramids surmounted by an upper temple, complete with frontal staircase. Yet the slope of these pyramids, which resemble those of Tikal on a reduced scale, approaches an angle of 80°. The ascending staircase is merely indicated by the motif of steps, for these are too narrow to use. In the same way, the small temple on the platform at the top is no more than a pretence; it has insufficient depth to contain a room. Nevertheless all the decorations typical of a pyramid and

The palace at Xpuhil: the three pyramids are crowned by sham upper temples

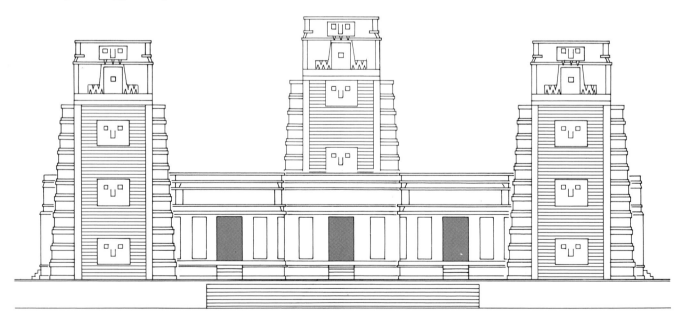

its upper temple can be identified in each of the three towers. Moreover, very narrow inner staircases, accommodated in the masonry of the towers, allow access to the roof-level of the palace.

Here the dominating horizontals and verticals are linked according to an original formula by which the pyramid becomes a purely symbolic shape, turned into a sham, its function lost.

Another noteworthy building in this intermediate series is the palace of Chacmultun in Yucatan which has four stages set on very wide superimposed terraces forming real esplanades between the different levels.

Clearly there is no lack of variation. Nevertheless, examples of buildings where the two elements of pyramid and palace are strictly differentiated remain far the most frequent.

Towers and Observatories

Buildings of a third type found in the Mayan cities have been classified by some experts as observatories. They are round or square towers whose function it is otherwise difficult to explain. Since the majority of texts and stelae refer to astronomical periods and dates, it is obvious that the calculations for the calendar, so important to the Mayan priests, must have been carried out in a predetermined place where it was easy to take measurements and sight lines.

In actual fact, the experts do not agree on this point either. Morley sees in the round tower of the Caracol at Chichen Itza an observatory whose three surviving loopholes allow one to determine the geographical south; the east and the sunrise at the equinox (March 21); and the positions of the moon at its setting at the northernmost and southernmost points also reached on March 21.

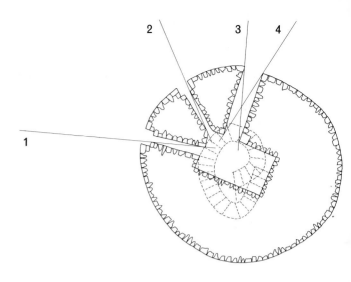

Plan of the upper chamber of the Caracol at Chichen Itza, used for astronomical observations (Morley). 1. Direction south; 2. Setting of the moon, March 21; 3. Direction west, and sunset at the equinoxes, March 21 and September 21; 4. Sunset on June 22, the summer solstice

Spinden, however, refuses to give credence to the theory that observatories existed among the Maya; according to him these buildings existed solely as places of worship. As proof, he points out that there are often higher buildings on the sites where these so-called observatories are erected. His argument, however, does not seem tenable, for at Chichen Itza, for example, the pyramid of the Castillo which is in fact the tallest building in the city, was obviously built at a later date than the Caracol. At Palenque, even if the Temple of the Inscriptions is slightly higher than the famous square tower dominating the palace, it is certainly less well situated for the taking of measurements. One could also be critical enough to add that the present situation in several European capitals also gives the lie to Spinden's views. For there the observatories are often lower than cathedral towers, for instance, yet it cannot be claimed that the observatory was there first.

The buildings used for astronomical measurements and calculations cannot be distinguished by any set of standard designs. Apparently each case was treated in a different manner. At Chichen Itza choice fell on a massive cylindrical tower, while at Palenque the tower is square, less heavy, and makes clever use of a staircase. Finally, at Uaxactun there is an architectural complex which, in Ricketson's opinion, allows the taking of sight lines.

It is true, however, that the three structures do not date from the same period. Uaxactun must be by far the earliest, the tower at Palenque dates from the last third of the eighth century and the Caracol at Chichen Itza from shortly before the decline of Mayan civilization in the late ninth or early tenth century.

This building, one of the last built by the Maya, is among those which offer best proof of their virtuosity as builders. The tower, 40 feet in diameter, rests on a quadrangular platform of 5,400 square feet which is again set on another platform with an area of 37,700 square feet. It is formed of two concentric rings and a cylindrical core. This results in the creation of two ring-shaped rooms which are vaulted in the classic Mayan style, here adapted, for the first and last time, to a circular plan unrelated to that of the primitive huts.

Within the central cylinder rises a winding stair giving access to the upper storey which contains a small room provided with observation loopholes, 80 feet above ground level. Caracol is the Spanish for snail and the building takes its name from the spiral described by the inner staircase.

A construction of such complex design could not, of course, merely derive from the imagination of its builders. Some functional use must have governed this structure with its annular vaults and fivefold doorways, its lofty chamber with loopholes, and its interplay of terraces and stairways on different axes. Furthermore, there are many representations of astronomical observations in the codices in which the observer is always shown in a stone chamber reached by means of staircases.

The Ball-Courts

A fourth type of building can be found in almost every town of any importance in Mayan territory and, indeed, in those of the other chief Central American civilizations. This is the ball-court, an immense form of gymnasium or sports ground.

These courts were the scene of original games which apparently had a religious significance similar to that of the Olympic Games of ancient Greece. The arena where the teams met was shaped like a double "T" or a very flattened "H". The game was played with a solid rubber ball and, according to the accounts of the early Spanish conquerors, its aim was to pass this through one of the stone rings set half-way between the two teams; these rings were fixed into the walls at each side of the center of the court, about 10 feet from the ground. Set vertically, at right angles to the wall, they fulfilled more or less the same function as the net baskets in the modern game of basket-ball, but as they are not to be found on all courts, it appears that the rules of the game varied from one city to another.

Triumphal Arches and Steam Baths

One of the most surprising features of Mayan architecture is a type of building, or rather monument, which archaeologists have termed a monumental gateway or triumphal arch in the Roman fashion. There are, it is true, comparatively few examples and they are in fact vaults usually serving as an architectural link between two blocks of buildings or two planned units. A particular case of this is at Labna where the vault is set as a corner link between two quadrangular groups of buildings. At Uxmal two arches originally joined the wings of the Palace of the Governor to the central block, though they did not perform the function of a passage. The most typical of these triumphal arches, however, is the one at Kabah: set in the perspective of an immense, rectilinear avenue, it resembles the monuments of the Roman Empire and seems to have a similar function.

One of the last types of building found in the cities of pure Mayan origin is the steam bath. These are small vaulted structures which seem to have been designed for use as Turkish baths. Their arrangement is often complex and includes heating apparatus whose purpose is to produce steam for the sudatoria and caldaria.

The existence of these baths built of masonry affords sufficient proof that stone architecture was also devoted to practical and functional ends, unless we accept the theory that these installations were used for religious rites.

From the Column to the Hypostyle Hall

At this point mention should be made of various Mexican contributions to Mayan architecture. The Itzas, the victorious warriors, who took over the Mayan civilization of Yucatan in the tenth century, rapidly assimilated the knowledge gained by their predecessors and combined the inheritance of the Maya with their own. Their largest contribution in the sphere of architecture concerned decoration, but an entirely new kind of spatial arrangement also made its appearance in their time: this was the hypostyle hall. It arose from their need to provide for gatherings of warriors, and, for this reason, was unknown in the time of the original Maya who had no need for buildings devoted to communal purposes.

The hypostyle hall, like that in the famous Temple of the Warriors at Chichen Itza, results from the combination of the Mayan vault, a form of construction unknown elsewhere in the pre-Columbian continent, with columns or pillars multiplied several times over and forming supports for the immense roofs.

Here it should be noted that the Maya were acquainted with both pillars and columns. We have already followed the development at Palenque, where the wall, pierced by openings set so close together as to produce a range of flat pillars, in effect resulted in a colonnade. This development continued in the north of the country and the first square or circular supports made their appearance in Yucatan round about the eighth century.

In fact, the column was unknown in the region of the Peten and, though the pillar was brought into use in the basin of the Usumacinta, the systematic use of a series of supports replacing walls pierced by doors developed only in the north.

The lower portion of the north wing of the Nunnery at Uxmal has two galleries on either side of the monumental staircase; these are supported on square pillars hewn from single blocks of stone whose bases resemble those of classical columns, but whose capitals are reduced to a square abacus. The next development was a cylindrical column; these were first executed in slabs of masonry as in buildings of the Rio Bec style, but, later on, the shaft was hewn from a single block and typified by a marked entasis. Here, too, a thick abacus did duty as a capital, but there was no base. This last type of column is found only in the Puuc region of northern Yucatan, at Kabah, Labna, Sayil and Chacmultun.

The chief innovation of Mayan-Toltec architecture lay in the use of these features. The Itzas combined the masonry vault of the Maya with the series of pillars and columns with which they were already familiar in their own territory, though there they used a simple covering of wood and thatch. At Chichen Itza, however, the Mayan vault does not rest on the walls, but on horizontal joists which are supported either by pillars or columns. Thus the rooms are made up of long parallel corridors, open to the façades.

In the lower part of the Temple of the Warriors the interior space consisted of four parallel bays running at right angles to the axis of the entrance. The rubble vaults supported by fifty or so square pillars represented a real architectural gamble, for their weight was enormous and the pillars were constructed of several superimposed blocks.

Nevertheless, this bold piece of construction had allowed the realization of a covered space measuring, in the first stage of its development, nearly 8,000 square feet. This was an immense advance on the largest covered areas of the Maya which hardly exceeded 860 square feet even in such exceptional cases as the big rooms in the center of the Palace of the Governor at Uxmal. In the vast Court of the Thousand Columns adjoining the Temple of the Warriors the hypostyle type of building increased its area to cover more than 14,000 square feet.

The difference between the interior spaces of the Maya and those of the Mexican immigrants was not merely quantitative: it was also qualitative. The Itzas who constructed interiors nearly 300 feet long by 50 wide were no less creative than the Arabs who built the hypostyle sanctuaries of the Omayyad mosques. The fact that both were inventions of warrior tribes is perhaps not entirely fortuitous.

An interesting factor that deserves to be stressed in the development of interior space at Chichen Itza is the transition from pillar to column. The early hypostyle halls have square pillars which, when seen in enfilade, give the impression of a wall surface. Buildings of a later period, however, including the Court of the Thousand Columns where the cylindrical shafts create cross views at an angle of $45°$ to the axes of the bays, form mazes where movement is possible in any direction. This results in an impression of freedom which the use of the pillar could not give. These vast, continuous covered spaces are the exact opposites of the Mayan chambers, although both have the same type of roofing.

Another development concerns the module of the columns, and the intercolumniation. At the palace of Sayil the shafts of the columns were no higher than three times their diameter; in the Court of the Thousand Columns at Chichen Itza, the relationship of the diameter of the column to its height was already one quarter, and at the Covered Market it became one-eighth. Similarly, though the spaces between the columns at Sayil were twice as high as wide, great efforts were made to enlarge the opening and increase the span of the lintels so as to give greater freedom of movement. Thus the proportion rose to 3:2 and the width of the intercolumniation changed from 3 to 8 feet.

It still remains to describe the curious covered market, resembling an impluvium, and a variety of monumental features such as stelae, altars, dancing platforms, bridges, underground aqueducts, roads and fortifications which complete the architectural vocabulary of the lands of the Maya. The majority of these are related to town-planning rather than to architecture as such and will be dealt with in the study devoted to the various cities and their basic characteristics.

Plates

Sayil (Yucatan)

113 **The Great Palace,** in the Puuc style, dating from the eighth-ninth centuries. The storeys are built in recession and the façade is divided by a wide staircase. The richly-ornamented first storey, its spacious openings supported by columns, forms a kind of piano nobile. The building contains about fifty chambers, arranged in double rows.

114 The western section of the building. The ground floor is almost completely destroyed, but the eastern lower portion and the first flight of the great staircase have recently been restored.

115 Detail of the engaged balusters, their triple swellings representing in stone the ties of wooden architecture.

116 The chambers of the first storey, their porticoes supported by bulging columns. The decorative scheme is based on a combination of small engaged columns ranging from the pedestal to the two moldings enclosing the balustered frieze.

117 A fine Chac mask decorating the frieze between two chambers. The row of teeth in high relief here assumes extraordinary importance.

Kabah (Yucatan)

118 The **Codz-Poop** or Palace of the Masks. The façade is covered with highly stylized masks of Chac one above the other, with long trunk-like noses, most of which are broken. The all-invading decoration of the Puuc style takes possession of the whole wall like the ornamentation of the Chenes style.

119 View along the façade pierced by five doors and enclosed between ornate moldings. On the extreme right, one of the few intact noses of Chac.

120 Detail of one of the 250 masks of the façade, each of which is composed of 30 sculptured elements. Thus, this stone mosaic consists of more than 7,500 finely-dressed blocks.

Labna (Yucatan)

121 **The triumphal arch.** Puuc style, eighth to ninth centuries. Its lofty vault forms a passage between two pieces of town planning. The mosaic decoration with its stylized huts and the grille representing an openwork screen resembles that of the Nunnery at Uxmal.

122 A geometrical mask surmounting an engaged column at a corner of the building. Eyes, mouth and ears are all represented in square form.

123 The east side of the monument. The decoration is a combination of engaged balusters and large Greek key-ornaments facing one another. On the top of the arch is a small openwork roof-comb.

Chichen Itza (Yucatan)

124 **The Nunnery.** (The end of this section brings together buildings at Chichen Itza in the Puuc and Chenes styles which are earlier than those of the Mexican or Toltec Period.) This façade, with its decoration reaching to the ground, is typical of the Chenes style. The door of the building, surmounted by fangs, represents the jaws of the god Chac, whose smaller-scale masks cover all the available surface.

125 The **Iglesia.** Although it is topped by a lofty openwork roof-comb, this small, one-roomed building adjoining the Nunnery belongs to the Puuc Period. It probably dates from the seventh to eighth centuries.

126 The **Caracol** (or "snail"). This cylindrical tower was the city's astronomical observatory. It is situated on a series of terraces and in its summit is a small chamber with loopholes for taking sight lines.

127 Detail of the observatory door. The tower is surrounded by a binder molding, and a mask of Chac dominating the entrance betrays the Puuc origins of the building which underwent frequent restorations in the Mexican Period.

128 On the summit of the Nunnery: the south façade of a storey added in the late Puuc Period. The geometrical decoration is here carried to extremes, but the roof recalls the mansard system so often used in the city of Palenque.

Great Palace, Sayil
Elevation and plan 1 :750 and detail of the first floor façade 1 :200

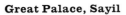

Palace of the
Elevation and p

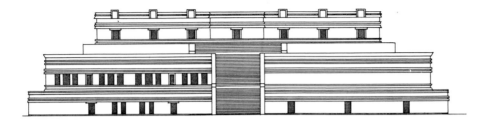

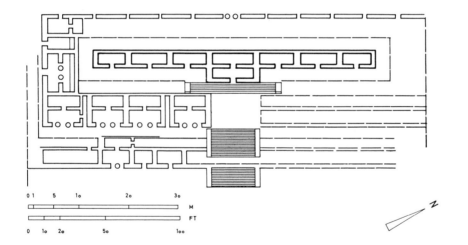

0 1   5   1o   2o   3o

M

FT

0   1o 2o   5o   1oo

N

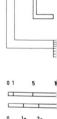

0 1   5

0   1o 2o

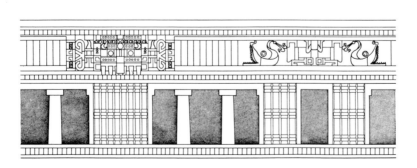

Codz-Poop, Kabah
and detail of one of the masks from the façade 1:20

Arch at Labna
Elevations of east and west faces, plan and section 1:200

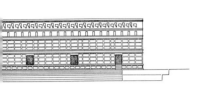

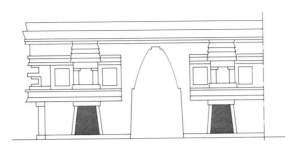

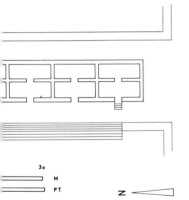

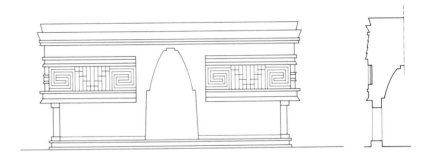

30

M

FT

100

N

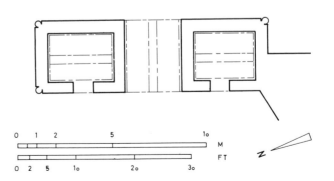

O 1 2   5   10   M

                                       FT

O 2 5   10   20   30

N

Notes

Sayil

A visit to the sites at Sayil and Labna can teach us a great deal about the Mayan architecture of Yucatan. To reach the ruins it is necessary to leave the road and advance through the scrub in a jeep, using mule tracks where progress is difficult. Only by doing this are we able to grasp the heavy population density of this region in the time of the ancient civilization. Everywhere there are traces of mounds submerged in the undergrowth and, every mile or so, remains of pyramids or small temples eaten away by the vegetation.

At a bend in the track we are confronted with a sight worthy of Cambodia: Santa Rosa Xlampak, an abandoned site in the middle of the forest, where a building in the Puuc style lies hidden among the creepers. Trees are firmly rooted in the ruined arches; their branches almost wholly conceal the cornice of the building and its frieze. Plants spring from the smallest cracks in the masks of Chac which ornament the corners, and are causing the gradual collapse of the individual features of the stone mosaic.

This temple remains in the state in which it was discovered in the scrub and shows what happened to these immense palaces before their ruins were completely cleared of vegetation and the work of restoration began. At Sayil, whole ranges of vaulted chambers have collapsed. The archaeologists have already reconstructed the ground floor of the east façade and the lower portion of the great staircase, and have also restored all the decorative motifs and friezes ornamenting the first storey, but much still remains to be done.

Kabah

The city of Kabah is one of the most important Mayan sites of the northern region. Many buildings have been discovered there, some of colossal proportions. Pyramids, palaces, courtyards and triumphal arches are scattered throughout the jungle at the mercy of a geographical setting more varied than in most of the other cities of Yucatan.

The most extraordinary, and also the best preserved building of this group is, without doubt, the Palace of Masks or Codz-Poop. One hundred and fifty feet long and twenty feet high, it is crowned by a small openwork roof-comb and is noteworthy for the great series of masks covering the whole façade. There must have been at least 240 altogether, but so far only the lower section of the building has been restored and there are hundreds of blocks on the ground awaiting the reconstruction of the frieze. In Mexico, about 15,000 important archaeological sites lie concealed, so it is obvious that the Instituto Nacional de Antropologia e Historia cannot undertake all this work at once.

Labna

A comparison of the photographic evidence of 1927 with the present state of the great arch of Labna confirms how carefully the archaeologists have proceeded with the work of restoration. In the first phase their aim was to prevent the building from crumbling away. The west front was reconstructed, leaving the eastern side in its original state. Latterly, the work has continued with the total reconstruction of the coping of the eastern face. There followed the restoration of the decorative motifs of the frieze and the re-cementing of the blocks which threatened to fall.

Chichen Itza

In the so-called Mayan section of Chichen Itza, it is not always easy to distinguish between the additions made to the buildings by the Mexican invaders and the features executed before the arrival of the Toltec tribes. Thus, the Caracol includes some Mayan terraces, but others have been added to, at a later date. The latter can be identified by their inclined walls, which resemble the pylons in Egyptian architecture.

Despite the destruction suffered by the tower of the Caracol, the preserved section has provided sufficient astronomical data for the archaeologists to conclude that this singularly complex building must have been an observatory where the priests took sight lines through the narrow loopholes of the upper chamber.

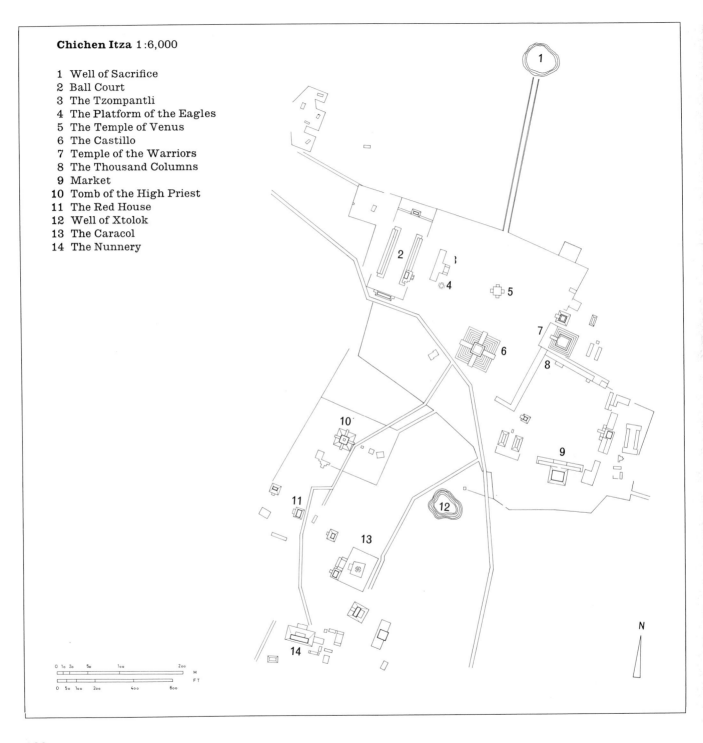

Chichen Itza 1:6,000

1 Well of Sacrifice
2 Ball Court
3 The Tzompantli
4 The Platform of the Eagles
5 The Temple of Venus
6 The Castillo
7 Temple of the Warriors
8 The Thousand Columns
9 Market
10 Tomb of the High Priest
11 The Red House
12 Well of Xtolok
13 The Caracol
14 The Nunnery

N

O 1o 2o   5o   1oo   2oo
M
F T
O 5o 1oo   2oo   4oo   6oo

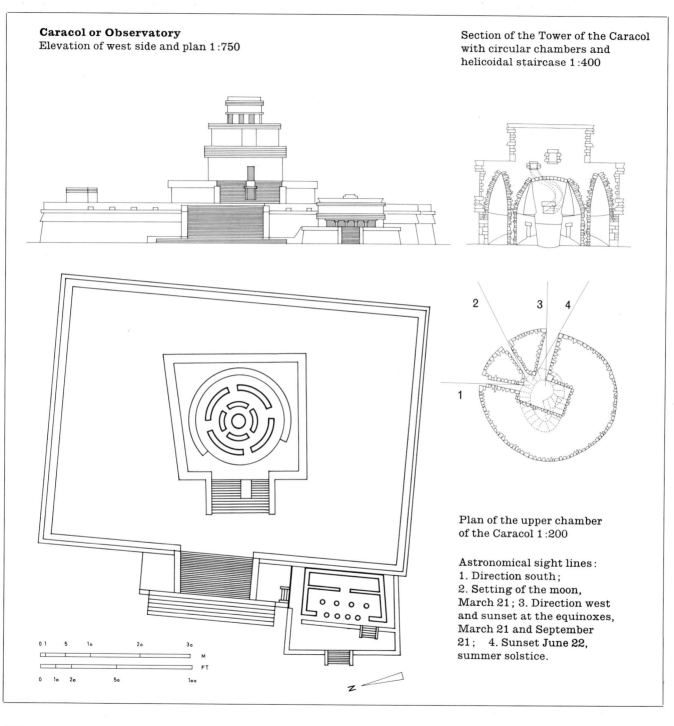

Caracol or Observatory
Elevation of west side and plan 1:750

Section of the Tower of the Caracol
with circular chambers and
helicoidal staircase 1:400

Plan of the upper chamber
of the Caracol 1:200

Astronomical sight lines:
1. Direction south;
2. Setting of the moon,
March 21; 3. Direction west
and sunset at the equinoxes,
March 21 and September
21; 4. Sunset June 22,
summer solstice.

3. Constructional Techniques and Decoration

The problems of technique raised by the architectural achievements of Mayan civilization must be considered in relation to the stage of development reached by the Indian population. For we must remember that the technical knowledge of the pre-Columbian period scarcely exceeded that of the neolithic age in Europe and was, in some respects, inferior to it. For instance, at the close of the neolithic age in the West, men had the use of domestic animals and the wheel or, at any rate, the potter's lathe. None of these things existed in the New World and their lack is all the more surprising when we consider that the architectural works of the Maya required almost superhuman resources.

The artificial terraces, esplanades and acropolises represent masses of materials often totaling several million tons and there are some monoliths, like the great statue of Quirigua, which weigh as much as 65 tons. Despite these vast weights, gigantic size is not a typical feature of Mayan architecture and its buildings have nothing in common with the megalithic style of Egypt in the time of the Pharaohs, Mycenaean Greece, or Peru.

Nevertheless, certain technical skills need explanation: the answers to the problems of technique provide valuable information on the disposition and division of labor in Mayan society.

Esplanades and Acropolises

Before they started to build their pyramids and palaces, the Maya provided them with monumental settings in the form of platforms and terraces. These colossal pedestals clearly have as much to do with town-planning as with architecture; they often provide a foundation for an entire complex of monuments.

This architectural feature, derived from the small platforms of the primitive huts, attains

131

astonishing proportions. At Copan, for instance, in its final stage of development, there is an artificial acropolis 125 feet high extending over twelve acres. It has a volume of over 70 million cubic feet and contains over five million tons of materials.

How were such accumulations of material possible in cities where there were only rudimentary methods of transport and no hoisting devices? There were no carts; nor were there cranes, winches and other tackle. All loads had either to be carried on men's backs or drawn on rollers made from logs.

It is difficult to envisage the work involved in the construction of the esplanade supporting the Governor's Palace at Uxmal, a level area 600 by 500 feet raised 40 feet off the ground. In all it involves some 12 million cubic feet of materials weighing nearly a million tons. Alberto Ruz reports the discovery of natural rock in the center of the esplanade, indicating that part of this small hill may be natural; even so, the dimensions of the platform remain colossal.

This building operation must be visualized as a ceaseless passage of workers carrying bales on their heads and back-baskets suspended from their shoulders. Each man would have carried a load of about 100 lb. on one journey which was probably no further than a mile or so.

Under these conditions he could have made two journeys an hour and, supposing that a day's work was between eight and ten hours, his daily contribution would have been about a ton. In all likelihood a minimum of 2,000 workmen at a time were allotted to this unskilled task and, in this case, the total daily load must have been about 2,000 tons.

This type of organization to which Mayan society was particularly suited, was conducive to a relatively high return. Nevertheless, if we deduct the periods of tropical rains which would have put a stop to all intensive labor, nearly two years must have been required merely to build the supports for a large building. Moreover time was essential to allow the masses of material to settle into a unified base sufficient to support a concrete building of considerable weight.

It should not be supposed that this construction at Uxmal was in any way exceptional or on a particularly gigantic scale. We have already noted that the acropolis at Copan was even larger, though it was realized in several stages possibly extending over the centuries.

The acropolis is seldom found in the lowlands of Yucatan. Instead, there are terraced esplanades. In the more mountainous region of Copan, however, the Mayan architects often carried out leveling operations, sometimes flattening out whole hills before starting on their buildings. This is so at Uaxactun and, to a certain extent, at Tikal.

Constructional Materials

Beaten earth played a prominent part in the foundations of Mayan buildings, but the early architects used chiefly wood, as was only natural in a country dominated by full-grown trees. To obtain the beams which they fashioned from the gigantic forest trees, often more than 100 feet high, they made use of fire or the cutting edge of flints which did less damage to the wood. They attacked the great acacias and sapodillas with polished axes of basalt or diorite and, later, with finer tools of obsidian, a substance which is fairly abundant in the volcanic highlands of Guatemala.

Attention has been drawn to the importance of the log structures in the thatched huts. The use of wood in stone buildings did not stop with

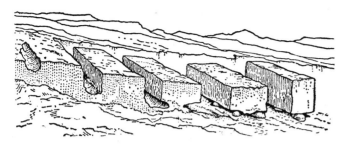

Method of extracting monoliths (Morley)

the lintels and fine ornamental bas-reliefs, the most beautiful example of which is the panel from Tikal now in the Ethnographic Museum at Basle. Wood was also constantly used in all constructional operations: for scaffolding and supports were essential to the building of vaults.

The Maya also used hammers made of flint to quarry the soft rocks which they needed for their buildings and their stelae. There are some unfinished works which show how the pre-Columbian peoples set about extracting the blocks from the quarries and how they carved the reliefs. Large stones such as the stelae which at Quirigua are nearly 36 feet high, were first of all made free standing by means of encircling cuttings. Next horizontal cuts were made below the block, level with the start of the vertical cuttings. Once it was freed the rectangular block was dragged along on wooden rollers by a team of men. On arrival at the site it was erected with the help of levers, one of its ends resting on a mound which was progressively raised to increase the vertical incline of the monolith.

It is comparatively easy to work on materials such as limestone and sandstone in the quarries where they are shielded from the air. After extraction, however, the stone dries and its hardness increases.

None of the stone buildings in Mayan territory

could have been constructed, however, without the use of cement. The Indians must have learnt how to extract lime at a very early period as the first examples of masonry date before the beginning of the Christian era.

How, then, did the Maya operate their lime-kilns? There is an abundance of limestone throughout the territories of the Peten, the Usumacinta and particularly Yucatan. Indeed, the present-day Indians still employ the method used by their ancestors. First they collect a large quantity of wood, which is piled up in the form of a cylinder, the height of a man, between 13 and 16 feet in diameter. The limestone is then crushed into pebbles no larger than a human fist and placed on this skilfully arranged pile of inflammable material. The stratum of limestone, some two feet thick, is first sprinkled with water to assist its decomposition. An upright piece of wood, set in the center, is withdrawn

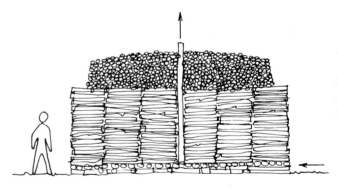

Mayan lime-kiln; the pieces of lime are set on top of a large heap of wood

when the fire is lit, thus creating a kind of chimney which causes a draught to circulate through the mass of limestone. The fire is kindled with the help of live embers and continues to burn for a whole day. At the end of the operation the lime forms a white, powdery heap, level with the ground. This has only to be mixed with crushed stones to obtain concrete, while mortar is produced by the addition of sand, though this is scarce in Mayan territory and marl usually takes its place.

The Maya made frequent use of stucco for the decoration and floors of their buildings. This was produced by means of plaster or a specially fine form of lime mixed with water which contained a solution of vegetable gum. The result was a substance resembling polished marble and, once dry, it became as hard as stone. Unfortunately the major defect of stucco in a tropical climate is deterioration when exposed to humidity, and, for this reason, there are few traces of bas-reliefs in this medium which have survived intact.

Foundations, Walls and Dressings

The bases of the buildings are often formed of beaten earth, but this would have been too light to act as a direct support for constructions of concrete. Thus the Maya were forced to lay heavier foundations as the weight and dimensions of their buildings increased. These foundations, however, never involved the digging of deep trenches. The usual type consisted of a bed of pebbles, sometimes overlaid with concrete, between half and one yard in depth. The surface

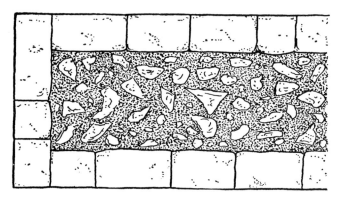

Structure of a wall at Copan: regularly-hewn blocks surround a concrete core (after Spinden)

was covered in stucco which formed the floors of the chambers and halls.

In the early days of stone construction, the Maya made their walls of fairly roughly hewn blocks held together by mortar. There followed a definite technical improvement which consisted of separating the two elements: the core of concrete or rubble was kept distinct from the facing. The blocks of stone were at first used as a very thick facing giving the impression of a uniform type of wall with regular courses and no concrete core. The horizontal courses were all approximately the same height. In time, the facing became thinner, until finally it was no more than a veneer, fulfilling no supporting function.

The stone blocks had to be carefully matched because they took the place of concrete casing, containing the liquid mortar poured between the two inner faces. The outer surface of the stone blocks was carefully dressed, but the inner facing in contact with the concrete was purposely left irregular so that the blocks might become completely integrated by means of a series of interlocking features.

The walls, and especially the vaults, of Copan kept throughout the typical stone age look of early Mayan architecture, where the balance between an inner rubble core and dressed stone is clearly in favor of the latter. In this case a small core of cement supports a double wall, but, in Yucatan, a thick concrete core is flanked by two finely-worked leaves of stone.

Different Types of Vaults

The development of masonry in Mayan wall structure is repeated in the case of the vault. This type of roofing has for long been considered a corbeled vault, but we have seen that even archaic buildings with their abundant use of flat slabs or well-matched stones set to overhang one

Types of Mayan vaults: 1. Classic vault of rough construction; 2. Vault with stone facing; 3. Bottle-shaped vault at Uaxactun; 4. Vault from the aqueduct at Palenque; 5. Vault with trilobe arch from the Palace at Palenque; 6. Concave vault from the Palace of the Governor at Uxmal (after Morley)

Others are convex or concave, while a third variety has the shape of a bottle in a sectional view: these begin by rising in a concave curve but straighten out again towards the summit to resemble the neck of a bottle. Finally, in the Palenque region, there are trilobe vaults whose strongly accentuated curves are reminiscent of Arab architecture. There is a particularly interesting use of this system in the buttress arches above the niches which line the corridors of the palace at Palenque. This is another case, however, where the original solution devised by the architects of the city does not seem to have been taken up elsewhere.

One characteristic of these vaults should be stressed: they are detached from the actual roof. This results in the creation of a form of entablature, both on the outside and inside walls, on which the vault and the frieze, if there is one, can rest. On the exterior this entablature often forms a band of molding which encircles the entire building at half its height and provides a strong horizontal accentuation.

To produce this type of vault and thinly-faced walls, the Maya obviously needed some kind of timber framework to keep the blocks of each course in place whilst the concrete was poured in. For this reason a tenon, which looked like a growth, was fixed on the rear side of each block. Embedded in the concrete, they prevented the stones from being dislodged by the downward thrust.

There must have been a particularly high risk of disaster in the actual course of construction of the vaults so long as the junction of the roof was unformed. The higher the courses rose, the greater was the increase of the overhang and the resulting lack of balance. Considerable time would have been needed for the construction of a vault: the facing could be applied only to two or three courses at most and the concrete molded.

another, would have collapsed under the combined thrust of the components. Thus the Mayan vault was evolved with the help of cement and rubble. At Copan, where the binding mortar is of inferior quality, the architects combined dressed stone with a concrete core in their vaults. One of the chief features of this city is the continued use of very fine material arranged in regular layers, the supporting role of which is more marked than elsewhere. The inner curve of the vault is often clearly cantilevered so that it resembles a double staircase turned upside down.

Though the Maya never wholly broke free from the prototype of the primitive huts and the height of their vaults usually exceeds their width, the forms of roofing are nevertheless varied in style. Some are simply composed of two plane surfaces linked by a horizontal ridge.

This operation must have been repeated several times as soon as the mortar set. In all probability, however, they did not wait for the mass to dry out and in this way were able to maintain the uniformity needed for correct cohesion between the different layers forming the concrete core.

In many cases there is evidence of cross-beams and, sometimes, of slabs spanning the vault half way up or at two levels, as at Palenque and Uxmal, where joists were placed at the base of the arch and, again, three-quarters of the way to the summit. The purpose of these features is not wholly constructional, although part of the internal scaffolding has been integrated with the building. In fact, some of these beams which are still in place prove from the way in which they are finished that they were intended for further use. At Tikal, for example, there are still some rounded joists ornamented with motifs resembling the stone balusters which decorate the façades of some of the palaces. They could have been sawn off once the mortar of the vault had finally set, had their presence not been required for some other purpose. Once the work was completed they played no further part as supports. There is yet another parallel between these beams and the tie rods forming the framework of the primitive huts: they were probably designed for the suspension of woven screens or the accommodation of objects of everyday use.

As walls became less heavy and facings more delicate, so the height of the vaults increased. At Copan they reached a height of 13 feet, and, at Palenque, 20, while, at Uxmal, the famous convex arches linking the wings of the Palace of the Governor to the center block reach a height of 25 feet.

The most advanced roofing systems in Mayan architecture are to be found in the Pyramid of Inscriptions at Palenque. Here an interior staircase descends 72 feet to ground level from the upper platform in two flights set in the heart of the masonry. This passage gives access to a funerary crypt unique of its kind. The construction of these vaulted staircases posed a new problem: how to roof a sloping space. The Mayan builders chose an unexpected solution. Instead of constructing one arch for each flight, whose angle of inclination would have been parallel to the movement of the ramp, they made a series of small vaults with horizontal ridges, so that the fall in level is halted by successive landings. This graded type of vaulting seems to have been discovered by the architects of Palenque.

The crypt itself uses the system of two vaulted transepts already noted in the Temple of the Sun in the same city. In this case, however, the primary area is that of the axis: the transepts scarcely project at all and serve as buttresses. Enormous stays of stone and masonry, high up in the main vault, prevent the sideways thrust threatened by the vast mass of the pyramid.

An extraordinary technical virtuosity is achieved in the Palenque region and there is evidence of brilliant innovations unparalleled elsewhere. Otherwise only the Mexican period of Chichen Itza and its hypostyle halls with their parallel vaulted bays seems capable of giving fresh impetus to the art of the pre-Columbian builders. Indeed, had the builders of Chichen Itza adopted the principle of the vaulted transepts of Palenque, and extended it on a large scale, a magnificent new form of interior space would have been produced. As it is, it seems that Mayan civilization became extinct at the very moment when this expansion was within its power.

Apart from the vault, there is another form of roofing, suitable only for small buildings, that must be briefly mentioned. This was a system of intersecting beams embedded in concrete which allowed the construction of flat roofs, lighter than the vaults. The process of erosion, however, soon caused the wooden props to rot and subsequent collapse has deprived us of almost all examples of this type.

Doorways and 'Ventilation Holes'

When the Maya wished to arrange an opening in the wall of a stone building, they adopted a very simple solution: they made a doorway. The doorways of their palaces and temples are square or rectangular and surmounted by a horizontal lintel designed to bear the weight of the roof. These openings are very seldom more than 8 feet high and often not more than 5 feet. If the lintel was more than 3 feet wide, it was executed in wood. This wood usually decayed in the course of centuries and brought widespread ruin to the buildings by its collapse.

Even in the finest stone monuments at Uxmal there is evidence of the survival of this early wooden feature. The lintels remained the only architectural features which were not translated into stone. It seems most likely that it was due to a form of traditionalism: their architects preferred to use wood rather than to advance boldly to the construction of a vaulted doorway.

When they used stone lintels, they narrowed the span of the opening as much as possible. There were two solutions to this problem. One was to incline the jambs slightly towards the center, as at Labna, where the trapezoidal shape of the door is very distinct. The other was to use intermediary columns as at the palace of Sayil with its fine first floor, rather on the pattern of an Italian piano nobile, whose colonnade is wide open to the exterior.

No Mayan entrance is provided with a door, for they relied on hangings to close the doorways of their temples and palaces. One unique exception, however, deserves mention. This is the triangular

doorway to the crypt at Palenque formed of a huge stone slab that can be made to pivot on itself. Here, too, the architects of Palenque showed their amazing inventive qualities.

Also at Palenque are found the best examples of tiny windows pierced in the walls, known by

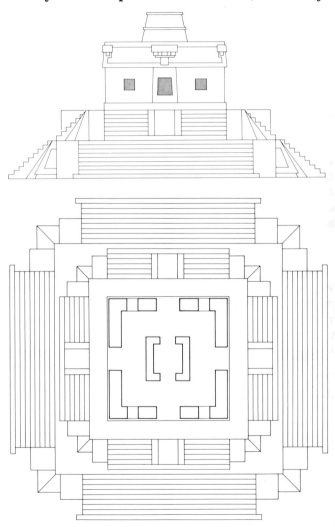

Temple I at Dzibilchaltun: constructed to a square plan with a roof-comb shaped like a truncated pyramid. The windows of this archaic building are unique in Mayan territory

archaeologists as 'ventilation holes'. With their baffling shape and miniature proportions, they are not really windows at all. They are more like loopholes, either square or T-shaped, pierced at a height of 5 feet above the level of the ground. Their function has not been clearly determined: the theory that they were a means of ventilation pays little heed to the traditional customs of the Maya.

The recently-discovered square windows, about 30 inches wide, on either side of the central doorway of the temple at Dzibilchaltun provide an interesting exception. This mysterious construction, composed of a series of planned features of unique type, dates from the fifth century and thus marks the beginnings of classic architecture in the northern Mayan territory. Perhaps this use of windows, unknown elsewhere, was finally lost, or perhaps it was restricted to this one site.

The Cresteria

Another typical feature of Mayan architecture are the high superstructures rising above the roofs to form a crest of stone and masonry: these decorative emblems translated into stone are known to archaeologists as cresteria or roof-combs. Here again, however, the discoveries made at Dzibilchaltun have perplexed the experts. For the square temple noted previously is surmounted by a kind of tower shaped like a lightly sloping truncated pyramid. This hollow tower, built of masonry, resembles the funnel of a chimney, except that it is closed at the top. It may be either a variation of the roof-comb or an adaptation to the square plan of this temple with its vaulted gallery. The second theory seems more plausible, but this cannot be settled until new discoveries shed more light on this point.

Whichever it may be, the roof-comb is of great importance. It is often higher than the building itself. Temple V at Tikal is topped by a crest

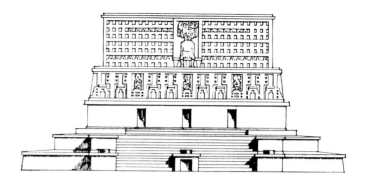

Yaxchilan: the lofty openwork roof-comb crowning the temple is decorated in high relief (after Marquina)

52 feet high, while the height of the sanctuary dominating the pyramid is no more than 30 feet.

The construction of this feature varies greatly according to region and period. At Tikal it is formed of masonry with gently sloping, stepped pyramidal faces. To support the vast weight of the roof-comb, the Maya set it over the back wall of the temple which was more solid and not weakened by the door opening.

The early roof-combs had smooth surfaces, but these were gradually covered with decorations in relief, as at Temple II at Tikal, where stucco masks and ornamental motifs add to its dignity. At Palenque the crest is changed into a double wall whose twin surfaces, their gentle slopes adorned with open work, are almost back to back and meet only at the summit. Later the crest is moved from the back wall to the center of the building where it rests on the partition wall. The delicacy of the open-work ornament is probably due not only to aesthetic reasons but also to more purely architectural considerations: a need to lighten and stabilize the structure and, at the same time, to offer less resistance to the wind. For these high curtain walls of stone often have a large surface area. Though at the temples of Palenque this is scarcely more than

540 square feet, it is doubled at the Temple of Quetzalcoatl at Yaxchilan. Here the decoration is especially remarkable, including a statue of the god in high relief, over 13 feet high. Finally, there is a curious series of open-work triangles surmounting the north wing of the House of Pigeons at Uxmal.

At Edzna the roof-comb is supported on the rear part of the building. At the pyramid of Labna, however, it is carried on the front wall. This last position is met again in the building known as the Iglesia at Chichen Itza where the highly complex frieze decoration is so prolonged as to change completely the proportions of the building. At the Red House in the same city there is a rare example of a double roof-comb, one above the façade wall, a second, higher, one above the partition wall.

With the finest buildings of the Puuc style the roof-comb disappears, after a transitional phase as a purely decorative projection surmounting doorways, as in the north wing of the Nunnery at Uxmal.

The development from the heavy crests crowning the temples of Tikal to the delicate open-work motifs of the House of the Pigeons at Uxmal, makes it clear that this feature increased in lightness, transparency and unreality before disappearing completely.

The Idea of Style in Mayan Architecture

In our analysis of the part played by the roof-combs, we have necessarily touched on the use of ornament in Mayan architecture. Their buildings, so extraordinarily sketchy in shape, size and interior space, are decorated with great richness and in a surprisingly varied manner. In some cases, exuberant motifs, thrusting movement and thematic invention have given rise to the expression 'Mayan Baroque'.

The decorative systems of the buildings change according to periods and regions. The archaeologists have classified these styles under various names. We have already noted the distinctions between the styles of Copan, the Peten and the valley of the Usumacinta in the south and center, those of Rio Bec, Chenes and Puuc in the north and, finally, the Mayan-Toltec or Mexican style of Chichen Itza. This idea of style should not be accepted in a restrictive context: in Mayan architecture it lies somewhere between regional variations and periods of history. Thus it can sometimes refer to the territorial localization of a typical theme, sometimes to the individual positioning of a decorative feature and sometimes to a stage of development in plastic expression.

It is the decorative elements, however, that demand our attention in a rapid enumeration of the essential characteristics of each of these Mayan styles: moldings, bas-reliefs, mosaics, sculpture, painting and polychromy. These help us to determine to what point Mayan architecture became an integrated form of art, and the different modes of expression fused into a complete unity. No feature dominates the others; they combine harmoniously without giving the impression that the decoration is merely an addition to the architecture. It is not a superficial surface movement, but one of the basic aspects of Mayan art.

Tikal and the Peten

At Tikal the bold lines of the pyramids combine with their compact heaviness to produce an astonishing effect; so does the consummate art with which the vast surfaces are subdivided into steps, whose moldings endlessly echo the slope of the roof and its disengagement from the wall. The sanctuary may be tiny and the temple's proportions may resemble those of a small fortress rather than a place of worship, but the roof-comb gives the whole building a look of lordly grandeur. Grotesque stucco masks, often taller than a man, endow the later buildings with a somewhat terrifying splendor. These masks, whose twitching faces, invariably repeated and transformed, cover the façades, are the product of a strange form of stylization which began to appear in the early stages of Mayan civilization. They usually represent either Chac, the rain god, or the celestial deity, Itzamna. It is clear that the surfaces were patterned geometrically from the start. The earliest reliefs decorating pyramid E VII at Uaxactun have a strange resemblance to those of the Olmec monoliths and depict mythical beings, part jaguar, part dragon, with curved fangs emerging from wide mouths, globular eyes, large ears, and horns.

This motif is found throughout the buildings of the Peten and Yucatan and is designed according to strict axial symmetry. The changes whereby each feature becomes stereotyped and the general arrangement and graphic treatment of the surfaces are ceaselessly modified, stem from laws adopted by other lands apart from that of the Maya. Indeed, they were known to many civilizations bordering the basin of the Pacific.

As the ethnologist, Claude Lévi-Strauss, has noted in his ''Structural Anthropology'', these fundamental, formal rules existed both in China in the second millennium B.C. and in nineteenth century Alaska and New Zealand; they are also present in Siberia and India. The almost complete resemblance between the masks that ornament the ritual bronze vessels of the Chang dynasty and the Chac masks of the Maya is extraordinary. The differences lie in scale and material. On the rounded surface of a vase the ornament measures only a few inches: a stone or stucco relief of monumental proportions can be as much as ten feet wide.

The masks of the temples of Tikal soon expanded into friezes covering the entire upper portions of the palaces. This use of endlessly repeated themes, which becomes obsessive with the Puuc style, is one of the fundamental rules of Mayan decoration.

In contrast to the massive sculptures of the buildings themselves, the bas-reliefs decorating the stelae — a common feature of the south — and the wooden panels within the sanctuaries, achieve an amazing complexity. Here, too, however, there is a very strict stylization in the arrangement of the motifs and the disposition of the figures. A characteristic of the entire central region is the contrast between the sober style of the buildings and the delicacy of the decoration carved in wood and stone.

Copan and its Statuary

In contrast to the art of the Peten, the influence of which can be distinguished in all the northern regional styles, Copan is typified by great originality. Its individuality is almost certainly due to its position away from the center.

Apart from bas-reliefs, Copan possesses a completely realistic free-standing sculpture of its own, unique of its kind. Examples of crude and highly schematic statues exist amongst the works of art of Yucatan, but nowhere else in the north is there a flowering of sculpture to equal that of Copan, apart from the Chac—Mool figures of the Mexican period whose prototypes were imported from Tula.

Similar stylized symmetry in a Chinese mask of the second millennium B.C. and a typical Chac mask of the Puuc style

On each side of the stairway leading to the Spectators' Gallery are monumental sculptures, representing the storm god kneeling in an attitude that combines servile obedience with terrifying power. Elsewhere flights of steps are bordered by jaguars rearing up on their hindpaws. The individual feature of this sculpture is that it is integrated so closely with the architecture that the courses of the building, formed of great blocks of green trachyte, continue across the figures with the utmost regularity. The unaccustomed character of such strange sculpture cannot be sufficiently stressed. Similar examples from other civilizations are rare, apart from the colossal figures of Osiris in the temples of the Pharaohs and the gigantic heads of Bayon at Angkor.

In this type of full-round sculpture, human proportions are respected and movement is carefully studied. This is far removed from the geometrical stylization eventually achieved by the masks. Thus, in its origins, Mayan sculpture was decidedly realistic.

This same interest in three-dimensional expression is also apparent in the treatment of stelae. At Copan and Quirigua, a city almost as far south and away from the center, figures on the monoliths are portrayed in high relief and are shown full face.

The City of Palenque

Nevertheless, the most naturalistic sculptures are to be found at Palenque. Here, the medium is not stone but stucco, from which the highly original artists of the city fashioned the finest miracles of Mayan sculpture. Particularly admirable examples are the heads discovered by Alberto Ruz in the crypt of the Pyramid of Inscriptions. The respect for truth dominating this art is quite overwhelming. The portraits move one by virtue of their simplicity and humanity, and they are unrivaled, save by the pure style of some Egyptian pieces dating from the Old Kingdom or the period of El Amarna.

More on a level with architecture are the magnificent stucco reliefs decorating the temples and palaces of the city. The pillars of the main palace were covered with rich decoration representing the chief Mayan dignitaries. A few traces of polychromy still survive on these decorations but, unfortunately, they have suffered severe damage from the humid atmosphere and the fires lit by the various eighteenth and nineteenth century expeditions to clear the site of its tangled vegetation.

The stuccoes of the Mayan palaces and temples should not be pictured as large areas of pale white. Originally they were brilliantly colored like the marbles of classical Greece and the granite sculptures of the Pharaohs. Today polychromy strikes us as barbarous, but it was the rule in all pre-Columbian civilizations as in those of ancient Europe.

The buildings, which now stand completely grey in the middle of the forest, did not originally have this austere, somewhat mournful look. On the contrary, radiant reds, greens, blues and yellows made a contrast with the surroundings which must have been extraordinary.

All the mansard roofs of Palenque were covered, on their sloping sides, with decorative reliefs, purely Baroque in style; every available inch was filled with ornament.

Within the temples low reliefs offered a sterner, more incisive type of decoration. They were interspersed with texts rather after the style of the hieroglyphs in the religious or secular scenes depicted in Egyptian tombs. Sometimes they formed part of the whole composition, sometimes actual pages of writing with each sign inscribed in a square.

141

Stucco was not the only material worked by the sculptors of Palenque: the formidable slab, several tons in weight, which covered the tomb of the priest-king buried in the Pyramid of Inscriptions was ornamented with a beautiful relief carved in the finest limestone. Similarly the sandstone stelae flanking the principal staircase of the main court of the palace show to what an extent the Maya had mastered the technique of sculpture and, especially, the level of freedom and invention attained by the style of Palenque.

The Rio Bec and Chenes Styles

With the buildings of the north, apart from the most ancient constructions whose characteristics are little known and often indistinguishable from those of the Peten, we deal with styles which flourished rather later than those of the central region. The great buildings of the cities of Tikal, Copan and Palenque date from between the fourth and eighth centuries, while the new styles in the peninsula of Yucatan came into being around A.D. 550 with those of Rio Bec, the Chenes and the Puuc. These reached their culminating point between the seventh and ninth centuries.

An obvious change of stylistic expression had already made itself felt round about the middle of the sixth century. The causes of these modifications are not known, but there is evidence that some features characteristic of the previous period, such as the hieroglyphic texts and the cult of the stelae, disappeared almost completely.

The southernmost of the three Yucatan styles is that of the Rio Bec which lies on the borders of the central region. This explains the towers shaped like the pyramids of Tikal which decorate the buildings of this branch of Mayan art. Certain features of the style, however, resemble those of the Chenes which borders the Rio Bec to the north; thus the mock temples crowning the artificial pyramids are completely covered with decorative motifs like the buildings of the Chenes. This decoration which covers the entire façade represents a huge mask, the mouth of which is formed by the doorway of the temple. It seems obvious that this devouring dragon must have been connected with some initiatory or divine rite.

The decorative reliefs on the towers of the Rio Bec buildings are constructed of faced masonry and combine two techniques: stucco and stone mosaic. This combination of rubble and a finely-dressed facing of stone opened the way to a new method of ornamentation. Originally the entire decoration was sculptured in stucco, but its vulnerability soon led the Maya to seek more lasting supports. To increase the solidity of their bas-reliefs the artists began to use stone elements which, to some extent, acted as a brace to the stucco. These stones, set in relief, soon came to form more and more complex combinations and finally became real mosaics.

A radical change of style derived from this technical development, for the use of stone necessarily imposed a certain stiffness of decoration. The free ornamental vocabulary which flourished at Palenque could not be translated into terms of the monumental mosaics which from now on covered temples and palaces. In this way Mayan decoration became progressively more geometrical. Supple stucco branches changed into right-angled key ornaments and human figures disappeared, yielding to an interplay of surfaces ornamented with the crosses, squares, bands, lozenges and checkerboard patterns typical of pre-Columbian art.

It was however in the mask theme representing either Chac or a dragon that the greatest development took place. This feature had always been executed with a strict, stylized simplicity and was thus well suited to the change made necessary by the substitution of materials. From now on there was to be a relentless march towards abstraction, leading by successive stages to the final elaboration where, reduced it to its simplest expression, the last representations of the mask motif are gone.

It is not easy to localize the creations of the Chenes style with any degree of precision. Its center certainly lay between the Rio Bec and the Puuc regions, and it expanded very far northwards. Radiating from Hochob, the style is again found at Uxmal in the western temple of the Pyramid of the Magician, and, at Chichen Itza in the façade of the extension to the Nunnery. Thus it reached the northern boundaries of Mayan territory.

The Puuc Style

The name Puuc, given to buildings in the northern zone, means 'land of low hills'; in fact, the limestone plateau of Yucatan is here as flat as a table top and, although slight undulations are visible here and there, the horizon line remains strictly rectilinear. Nevertheless, the region must have been particularly fertile, for it is one of the richest in Mayan architectural remains.

The basic differences between the Chenes and the Puuc styles lie in two easily identifiable characteristics. First of all, in place of the façades covered with stylized ornament unique to the Chenes, the Puuc buildings offer smooth walls surmounted by decorated friezes. Secondly, between the wall and its band of vertical ornamentation, a wide molding completely surrounds the building. Mexican writers refer to this as the moldura de atadura or binder molding. There is also a similar motif in the form of a cornice at the summit of the building. This form of double girdle surrounding the upper portion of the building, acting as a border to the frieze, derives from the linking cords which served to strength-en the walls of the thatched huts. Here again, as with most of the structural elements of Mayan architecture, it is a case of translation into stone.

Another example of this is found in one of the favorite themes of Puuc decoration: the rows of engaged balusters ornamenting the friezes of certain buildings. This form of decoration is based on the repetition of a motif of round logs placed upright, side by side, and occurs in parts of the quadrangle of the Nunnery and in the fine House of the Tortoises at Uxmal, on the upper storeys of the great palace of Sayil, in one of the palaces at Labna, and elsewhere.

Strangely enough there is evidence of a similar motif, resembling a latticed opening, on the far shore of the Pacific. This decorative theme, integrated with wall elements, can be found in Khmer buildings, especially at Angkor Vat. Thousands of miles away the same phenomena give rise to the same transpositions: round balusters, inspired by early wood constructions, survive in stone, but no longer fulfil their original function.

The masks of Chac and the celestial dragon, however, remain the most frequently used decorative elements of the Puuc style. Yucatec ornament is standardized on this point, but, though the Puuc lies in a direct line with Rio Bec and the Chenes, the mask no longer covers the whole façade. It becomes smaller, but is endlessly repeated. Here too there is clear proof of the liking of the Maya for the rhythmic repetition of a theme. The Puuc was more strongly influenced by geometry than the Rio Bec or the Chenes.

This led to an extreme formal simplicity, reducing motifs to their essential lines, and going so far as to render the early figurative images unrecognizable.

Mass Production

Thus the two chief influences on the formation of the Puuc decorative style were repetition and geometrical forms. These two factors combined to make the art of Yucatan into one of the most spectacular examples of large-scale mass-produced architectural work. A good example is the Palace of the Governor at Uxmal. This vast building, nearly 300 feet long, is surmounted by a huge mosaic frieze, with decoration 10 feet high which surrounds the entire construction. Its surface area is about 7,500 square feet. A careful study of the elements of the decoration reveals that each stone is between 8 and 24 inches in length and weighs between 55 and 175 pounds. There are about 150 masks of Chac not more than 3 feet wide and $27\frac{1}{2}$ inches high. The large Greek key patterns symbolizing the serpent in the Mayan pantheon extend over an area of more than 16 square feet and consist of 40 elements.

There are 150 masks divided between the four faces of the building and these account for 300 eyes, 300 horns, 300 hooked fangs and 300 ears each formed of two blocks to assist the perforation, making 600 pieces. The whole composition consists of 20,000 blocks, more than half of which are attached to the single cross-piece forming the background from which the decorative motifs stand out.

What is the meaning of these large quantities of similar features? We must remember that these elements were inserted with unparalleled accuracy, for they form facing as well as ornamentation and, furthermore, act as containers for the concrete. Thus the courses could not be loose fitting, though there is evidence of differences between blocks which are theoretically of similar dimensions, and it is possible to note some ingenious corrections. This does not often occur, however. Indeed, it would have been impossible to continue with the construction of

Cross-bars imitating a grating: (a) As realized by the Mayan builders (b) As they should have been arranged to place the vertical joins in alternation

the frieze, had the margin of error been much more than a third of an inch per element. More variations can be found in the sculptured motifs, where ornamental differences were less vital.

Analysis of the composition of the stone cross-piece (which must contain more than 10,000 identical pieces) makes it apparent that this grid is formed by the juxtaposition of square blocks bearing on their faces a relief decoration in the shape of a St Andrew's cross. Obviously, the slightest inaccuracy repeated on this vast number of copies could have had disastrous results on the distribution and proportion of the decoration. In this regard it may seem strange that the Maya did not arrange the elements of this stone trellis in groups of five; because of the constant level of the courses, it would have been easy to make symmetrical joins in the same way as in walls with regular courses. The arrangement actually adopted resulted in a succession of vertical joins extending the height of the motif. This solution does not cause a weakening of the facing as it plays no part in carrying the weight of the building, but, nevertheless, it appears absurd at first sight and contradictory to every architectural convention. To obtain the same visual effect, it would have been enough to alternate two types of block—those carved with the motif of the St Andrew's cross and those with a square hollowed out in the center. This system, however, would have brought further difficulties. It would have been necessary to allow for half blocks on the edges of the motifs and would have involved three series of elements in the place of one. It seems that here the rationalization of work and the choice of the most economical solution took precedence over tradition in the eyes of the Mayan architects.

The workshops of the stone-cutters and sculptors must have operated according to a system of prefabrication. All the evidence leads to the conclusion that the Maya possessed an organization working in accordance with our idea of mass-production. Teams were allotted to rough-hew thousands of identical blocks which were then dressed regularly on five faces. These preliminary efforts were then passed to teams of sculptors who again had to parcel out the work amongst themselves. The inexperienced artisans worked only on simple, unornamented geometrical forms, while the more talented craftsmen were engaged on the reliefs of the sculptured features. Only a method such as this could have led to the successful results we see today.

Amongst a people scarcely advanced beyond the neolithic period, it is amazing to come across solutions heralding such modern industrial techniques as prefabrication, mass-production and the rationalization of labor. In the social field, the consequences must clearly have been considerable. Observations of this kind teach us more about the structure of Mayan society than a whole host of sociological treatises.

Such constructional methods would suggest the existence of a strict, centralized organization and a system of dictatorship. Apparently, however, liberty was not wanting in this art, and the best proof of the comparative independence existing in the different regions of Mayan territory lies in the variety of local styles. Thus there is no question of a powerful political group, for the cities maintain their marked individuality, even though they are very close to one another. On the other hand, it seems highly probable that the priests and nobles had absolute power over the peasants and artisans as in medieval Europe, but the authority of this governing caste can hardly have extended beyond a small group of cities. For this reason regional differences never yielded to general uniformity as might have been supposed from the idea of mass-production.

Mayan forms of expression are so varied that combinations of styles frequently occur. At Kabah, the Codz-Poop lies half way between the Chenes and Puuc styles; this is a fascinating palace 150 feet in length with a façade 20 feet high so completely covered by 250 masks that there is no smooth surface left on the wall pierced by five doors. The stylized masks derive from the Puuc and the covering decoration that extends to ground level from the Chenes. We may note that each of the 250 masks is formed of 30 elements, amounting to 7,500 finely hewn stones. This rich decoration heralds the flowering of the Colonial Baroque style whose sumptuous churches were later to adorn the New World.

Despite these remarks on diversity, we must not lose sight of the characteristics which help us to identify the principal buildings of the Puuc style: the use of a thin facing, façades surmounted by a vertical frieze interrupted by the binder molding, the appearance of columns, geometrical motifs, and stone mosaic replacing stucco.

Color was also an important feature of all Puuc buildings. Red backgrounds and green motifs contrasted with the whiteness of the stone which was often heightened by whitewash or a very fine coating of liquid stucco.

The Mayan-Toltec or Mexican Style

The last of the Mayan styles developed in the sacred city of Chichen Itza, yet it is somewhat misleading to attach it to the native civilization of Yucatan; it came into being there only as the result of a synthesis between Mayan techniques and the art of the Itzas, the Toltec invaders. On their arrival in the ancient city of Chichen Itza, which they were to make the central point of their influence on northern Yucatan, the invaders found some beautiful examples of Puuc and Chenes architecture.

The union of the Mayan civilization and that of the newcomers from Tula resulted in such a perfect synthesis that the experts cannot agree on a chronology for the buildings of Chichen Itza; some seek to include the Caracol among the Toltec constructions whilst others rightly see it as a Mayan building with later alterations. The following sequence appears to be correct: the Nunnery, the Iglesia, the extension to the Nunnery, the Caracol; then, about the middle of the tenth century, came the invasion of the Itzas who shortly afterwards built the first Castillo and the Temple of the Warriors; simultaneously they made alterations to the Caracol and the east wing of the Nunnery and afterwards built the Court of the Thousand Columns, the second Castillo and the great ball-court. Their period of power at Chichen Itza extended from 950 to about 1200.

Naturally, this incursion of foreign elements provoked a real revolution in Mayan art and architecture.

The extent of this transformation was such that Chichen Itza has more in common with the decorative art of Tula than that of the Maya. The plans of the Temple of the Warriors at Chichen and Building B at Tula are completely identical: they have the same entrance colonnades, the same monumental stairways, the same stepped pyramidal structures, the same friezes representing prowling tigers and eagles devouring hearts, and the same columns in the form of serpents. There is complete similarity, apart from the basic contribution of the Maya: the masonry vault from which the Itzas profited to a remarkable extent, as we have already noted, in the erection of their hypostyle halls.

In the field of ornament, Mayan-Toltec art has many characteristic features, the chief of which are: motifs of plumed serpents and monumental columns bearing their effigies in high relief; great statues representing recumbent human figures, resting on their shoulders, which have come to be known as Chac-Mool; stone altars sculptured in the form of jaguars, tigers, eagles and death's heads carved in low relief on friezes; warriors decorating the four faces of the pillars in the hypostyle halls; the life-size caryatids, of Chichen Itza Viejo, and the little atlantean figures supporting the altar in the Temple of the Warriors; the standard-bearers on either side of the monumental stairways; and, lastly, a very individual element, the sloping embankments below the walls.

Almost all these features derive directly from Tula which, in its turn, had often inherited them from the civilizations of Teotihuacan, Tajin and the Zapotecs. Thus Mayan-Toltec art can be described as Mexican; for it reflects a great unifying movement as the result of which the widely diverse currents of various pre-Columbian cultures meet and fuse.

Plates

Chichen Itza (Yucatan)

151 **The Castillo.** Like all the buildings of the Mexican or Toltec Period at Chichen Itza, this magnificent construction dates from the tenth or eleventh centuries A.D. It is a great step pyramid flanked by four staircases bordered by ramps, and surmounted by a perfectly preserved upper temple. Left: the Temple of the Warriors and the Court of the Thousand Columns.

152 The pyramid from the Temple of the Warriors. The right-hand section has been completely reconstituted by the archaeologists, but the left-hand one is still in a ruinous state. The building is 180 feet long and 100 feet high. Each staircase has 91 steps, making 364 in all. An extra one at the entrance to the upper temple brings the total up to 365, the number of days in the year. The plumed serpents' heads represent the god Kukulkan.

154 The pyramid. In the foreground, a staircase of the quadrangular platform known as the Temple of Venus. At the top of the ramps are plumed serpents with open jaws.

155 The great Chac-Mool from the secret chamber of the Castillo. It is a fully detached figure, stretched out and resting on its elbows, on which the priests probably placed their offerings. In the background is the throne of the red jaguar inlaid with jade.

156 **The Temple of the Warriors** preceded by the Court of the Thousand Columns. The roofs of the building and the colonnade have disappeared.

158 Column in the form of a serpent at the entrance to the sanctuary. The jaws of Kukulkan are open at ground level, while the serpent's body forms the shaft. On the façade are masks of Chac with their trunk-shaped noses.

159 At the top of the staircases leading to the sanctuary: plumed serpent and standard bearer.

160 Bas-relief from one of the square pillars in front of the temple. It shows a 'Mexican' warrior with a plumed headdress.

161 Cylindrical columns of superimposed drums, crowned with a square abacus, which supported the parallel vaults of the "Thousand Columns".

162 Square pillars of the sanctuary dominating the Temple of the Warriors. In the center, the Chac-Mool figure at the top of the stairways. Beyond, the Ball-Court.

163 **Platform of the Eagles.** This monument resembles the so-called Temple of Venus and is decorated with bas-reliefs representing eagles devouring hearts, jaguars, plumed serpents, and warriors.

164 **The Ball-Court** from the summit of the Castillo. On the left, the South Temple. On the right is the Temple of the Tigers; it consists of a lower sanctuary opening on to the square, and an upper temple facing the interior of the Ball-Court.

165 A 'Mexican' warrior from the lower Temple of the Tigers. He carries a shield and an obsidian-headed javelin and wears a plumed headdress.

166 The Temple of the Tigers. Plumed serpents' heads rise from the corners of the truncated pyramid.

167 The lower section of the temple. At the entrance, a tiger forms an altar. In this building of the Mexican period are clear traces of the binder-moldings of Mayan architecture.

168 Inside the Ball-Court with the North Temple in the background of the enclosure. In the middle of the vertical wall is the stone ring through which the rubber ball had to pass.

169 Skull in low-relief on the retaining wall of the Ball-Court. This symbol of death haunted Mayan-Toltec civilization. Human sacrifices involving the cutting out of the heart became increasingly frequent.

170 The **Tzompantli** or Skull-rack. The skulls decorating the faces of this great rectangular platform, 200 feet in length, clearly indicate the function of this monument: the skulls of enemies were there offered in solemn sacrifice to the god Kukulkan.

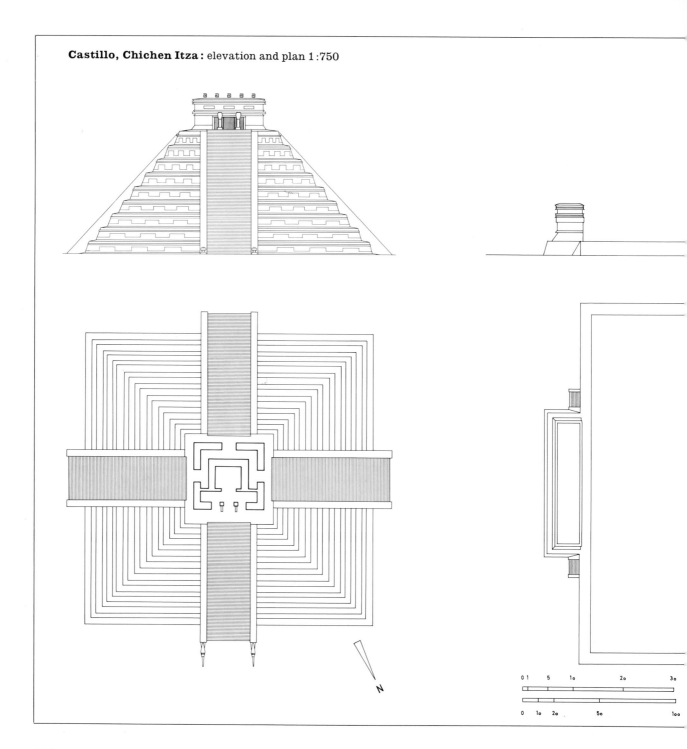

Castillo, Chichen Itza: elevation and plan 1:750

0 1   5   1o   2o   3o

0   1o 2o   5o   1oo

N

Great Ball Court, Chichen Itza : elevation and plan 1 :750

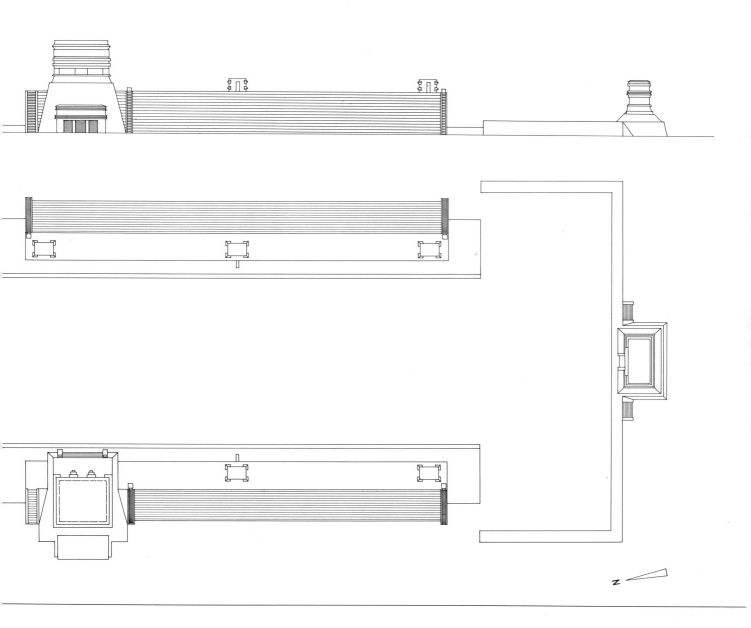

149

Notes

Chichen Itza (Mexican Period)

The great city of Chichen Itza was one of the first to be excavated in the New World, the Mexican government taking steps to preserve the site in 1906. Between 1923 and 1943, the Carnegie Institution, Washington, in collaboration with the Mexican Ministry of Education set out to reconstruct several of the buildings, under the direction of Sylvanus Morley.

The Castillo

The primary aim of the excavations at the Castillo was to restore two of the faces of this imposing building to their pristine beauty. Comparison of these with the other two allow us to appreciate the success of the work. It was not long, however, before the archaeologists realized that the pyramid enclosed another, earlier one. Superimpositions of this kind occur so frequently in the Mayan world that it is now usual to make trial bores to throw light on a building's history. In this case the investigators were amazed when they discovered, beneath the visible sanctuary on the summit of the pyramid, another upper temple literally imprisoned intact inside the massive construction.

Within this chamber, unvisited by man for close on a thousand years, the archaeologists set eyes on a sanctuary in the state in which the priests had left it after their last ceremony. Stretched across the threshold was a great Chac-Mool figure and, behind it, stood the throne of the red jaguar. This painted stone statue, representing a life-size jaguar, is decorated with 73 pieces of jade inlay simulating the beast's speckled hide. Real animal teeth are set in his threatening, open jaws and his eyes are represented by two jade balls.

The Temple of the Warriors

When excavations were begun among the heap of rubble to which the Temple of the Warriors with its fallen vaults had been reduced, just as at the Castillo, a substructure was discovered similar to the visible building, though on a smaller scale. This temple which dates from the early Toltec Period, contains columns, paintings, and a very interesting Chac-Mool figure.

In the case of the bigger temple, the collapse of the stone ceilings necessitated large-scale works. Its parallel aisles, which were supported by wooden planks, had been devised by the new arrivals from a combination of the Mayan system and the formula of the colonnade peculiar to the buildings of Tula, in order to create vast hypostyle halls. When the beams decayed, they dragged down the entire masonry vaults in their fall.

The Sacred Well

The site of Chichen Itza includes two vast natural wells. These openings in the limestone of Yucatan are between 165 and 200 feet in diameter and have a depth of some 65 feet to the surface of the water. One of them was used as a reservoir for the community living nearby; the other played a religious part. With the arrival of the Toltecs worship was offered to the god Tlaloc, the divinity of rain adopted by the peoples of the central Mexican plateau. During periods of drought, young men and women were sacrificed in the well to conciliate the god. The victims were thrown alive with all their jewels into the water which was between 10 and 40 feet deep, to perish by drowning.

These traditions, which were recorded by Bishop Landa in the sixteenth century, led the archaeologist Thompson to drag the muddy bed of the well. From it he withdrew a large number of objects now exhibited in the Peabody Museum at Harvard University. They include pieces of jade, carved shells, copal balls, stone weapons and several examples of gold and copper jewellery: rings, necklaces, bracelets, pendants, earrings and gold discs ornamented with repousse motifs. Most of these pieces of metal come from non-Mayan regions and are of a late date (thirteenth to sixteenth centuries).

Fresh discoveries have just been made in this well by a team of Mexican and American frogmen who have gathered a rich harvest of documentary evidence. Thus a highly modern technique has assisted the archaeologists to produce fresh information regarding the mysterious pre-Columbian civilizations.

The Thousand Columns, Chichen Itza 1:2,000

1 Temple of the Warriors
2 North-east colonnade
3 Ball court
4 Covered market
5 Ball court
6 Steam bath

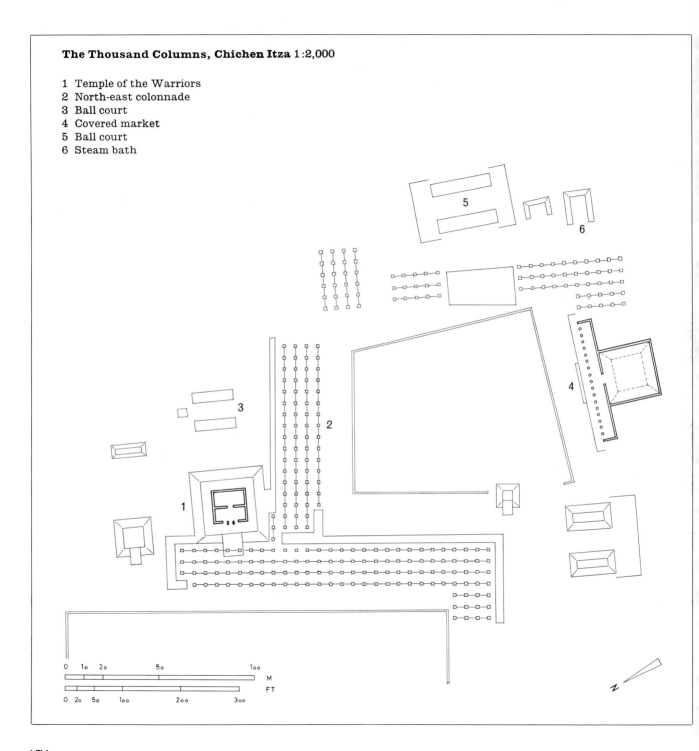

O   1o 2o   5o   1oo   M

0 2o 5o   1oo   2oo   3oo   FT

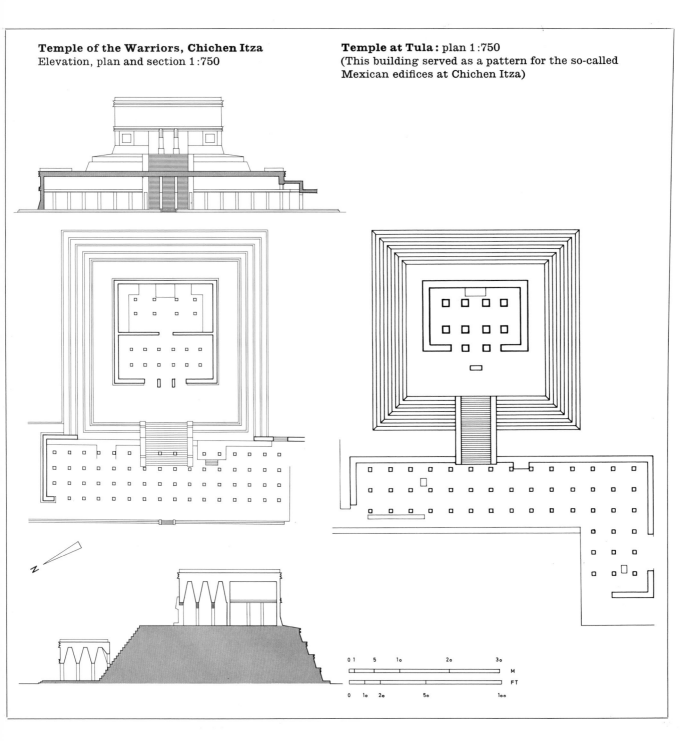

Temple of the Warriors, Chichen Itza
Elevation, plan and section 1:750

Temple at Tula: plan 1:750
(This building served as a pattern for the so-called
Mexican edifices at Chichen Itza)

0 1   5   1o   2o   3o   M

0   1o   2o   5o   1oo   FT

4. Architectural and Urban Spaces

We must now analyze the methods of composition individual to Mayan architecture and the sculptural expression inherent in their buildings and town planning.

First, the development of forms and spaces. We have already seen that throughout the five or six centuries of Mayan architecture's evolution the various types of monuments did not abide by a fixed set of rules. An almost dynamic development of forms manifests itself, in spite of an early rigidity of interior space. These changes are apparent from the layout of the buildings: walls grow progressively thinner, the chambers somewhat larger; their combinations become more complicated and they expand on a more generous scale. Moreover, the palaces are freed from the artificial hills and acropolises to which they had long been attached. In the case of elevations and façades increasing stress is laid on the interplay of masses: vaults become progressively higher and, with the passage of time, there is a search for continuity, for a more confident language. Despite the breaking up of the interior spaces the buildings seem, from the exterior, completely unified: the constituent parts and the façade are dissociated. The cells are literally submerged in the play of the masses which go to make up the grandiose perspectives.

Apart from this development, there exists a series of rules governing the erection of stone buildings. The arrangement of the plans and the elevations of façades betray an overwhelming preoccupation with right angles. The combination of horizontals and verticals is also evident in decorative details and in the treatment of large surfaces.

Another fundamental element is the need for symmetry which is revealed in the plans of buildings and their elevations: the reflected symmetry of façades, the axial symmetry of the pyramids and the double vertical symmetry of

173

the temples with four staircases, like those at Uaxactun and Chichen Itza. This compositional law, which can be found in all antique civilizations and derives from the structure of the face, of man, animals, insects and, indeed, of all complex biological organisms, is by no means synonymous with monotony: it possesses an infinite diversity, an exemplary flexibility.

An attempt to discover the rhythm governing the composition of a façade such as the Palace of the Governor at Uxmal may serve as proof. We should try to establish its key plan in order to understand how expert the Maya were in the interplay of detail. They were continually avoiding the exaggeratedly simple rhythm of an unchanging series of repetitions. The subtle composition and the relationship of solids to space cannot be calculated in simple arithmetic any more than the proportions can be transcribed into common fractions.

Similar care can be found in the ornamentation and the relationship between the various decorative elements such as friezes, moldings and cornices. Thus the binder molding of the House of Tortoises is so conceived as to offer exactly the same profile as the cornice surmounting the building; but the relationship between the width of these two bands is infinitely complex both with regard to their sections and the distribution of the beveled planes of which they are composed.

Superimposed Buildings

The most constant, the strangest and most revealing of the Mayan building laws—one which is shared by the chief Central American cultures of the pre-Columbian period—is the rule of superimposition. The majority of their buildings are the products of a series of constructions each of which includes the one before. For this reason, when archaeologists wish to know the date of occupation of a site, they turn their attention to the construction to see how

many other buildings it contains concealed within one another. Thus, beneath the structure A-V at Uaxactun, the excavations have revealed a series of seven previous states which grow smaller the further they go back in time.

This rule of superimposition has provided the archaeologists with much invaluable information. Not only does it enable the evolution of a building to be traced over the different stages of its existence, but it often reveals a second smaller pyramid in a perfect state of preservation beneath one which is completely ruined. A particular example of this is the structure G-VII at Uaxactun; excavations revealed its facing of white stucco just as it must have been erected 2,000 years ago. Shortly afterwards this amazing discovery was reduced to a shapeless heap of materials. The rain and the vegetation attacked it on all sides and a few years sufficed to annihilate a masterpiece which had survived for centuries sheltered from the destructive elements of nature.

Other discoveries have been made thanks to this particular custom and to the almost sacrosanct respect accorded by the Maya to their building sites. These superimpositions have made it possible to determine the succession of styles and the development of constructional

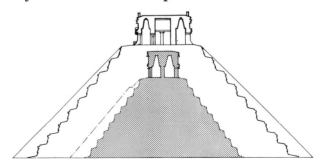

Section of the Castillo at Chichen Itza showing the two superimposed buildings: the first pyramid has been rediscovered beneath the masonry of the second (after Marquina)

techniques. Thus the Castillo at Chichen Itza contains a second much smaller pyramid whose upper temple survives complete beneath the platform of the visible building. This is one of the earliest Toltec structures in Yucatan. When the archaeologists opened the sanctuary, they discovered a throne in the shape of a jaguar painted red and incrusted with jade plaques, together with a fine Chac-Mool set before the earlier entrance at the top of the ancient stairs. Beneath the masonry of the outer pyramid they also found the previous façade with its sculptured decoration of prowling tigers.

The Pyramid of the Magician at Uxmal is also the result of several superimpositions. The first sanctuary lies on the western side almost at ground level; above it on the other side of the building, three-quarters of the way up the eastern staircase, is another temple. A third temple stands on the western side, at the same level as the preceding one. This was finally provided with a narthex characterized by a façade in the Chenes style which is still visible at the top of the staircase bordered by the masks of Chac. On the other side a new staircase covers the earlier one and leads to a final temple well above the level of the others because the roof-comb dominating Temple II is buried in the masonry.

Other changes can result from these superimpositions. For example, such additions may account for the presence of two chambers one behind the other; or for galleries with columns built in front of a range of old style chambers; or terraces enlarging the base of a building and incorporating the original foundations.

From some points of view this Mayan tradition of enlarging buildings while allowing the previous structures to survive is comparable with the modern idea of organic growth. In the case of group A-V at Uaxactun, for instance, it is possible to follow every stage of its progressive enlargement combining the system of superimposition with a real form of extension. The complexity of the spatial structure advances steadily till it reaches a final stage, characterized by four main buildings enclosing a small courtyard. This arrangement has scarcely any connection with the three original pyramids set in the shape of a horseshoe. The spatial organization has undergone a series of radical transformations which offer abundant proof of formal evolution. There are clear traces of components embedded in new constructions, of countless additions and elevations, and of basic modifications which have rendered the intermediary states completely unrecognizable. From the fusion of three small sanctuaries with roof-combs occupying the same site, there develops one long palace whose horizontal lines have nothing in common with the threefold vertical accentuation of the earlier structure.

The Sculptural Expression of Buildings

Seen through modern eyes Mayan architecture reveals a coherence of method which allows more and more complex combinations to follow one another. The sequence leads from ornamental mosaics to town-planning by way of individual buildings and groups of buildings inserted into an urban pattern. The building up of the detail is as assured as that of the groups, but it is necessary to lay special stress on the part played by two essential components: the powerful light and the large scale of the exterior spaces. These two factors literally shape the face of Mayan architecture.

Thus the mosaic reliefs of the Puuc style palaces are as much ornamental motifs as pure sculpture. The Maya made remarkably clever use of the sun's angle of incidence; for, in tropical latitudes, the slightest projection is responsible for very deep shadows. Nevertheless

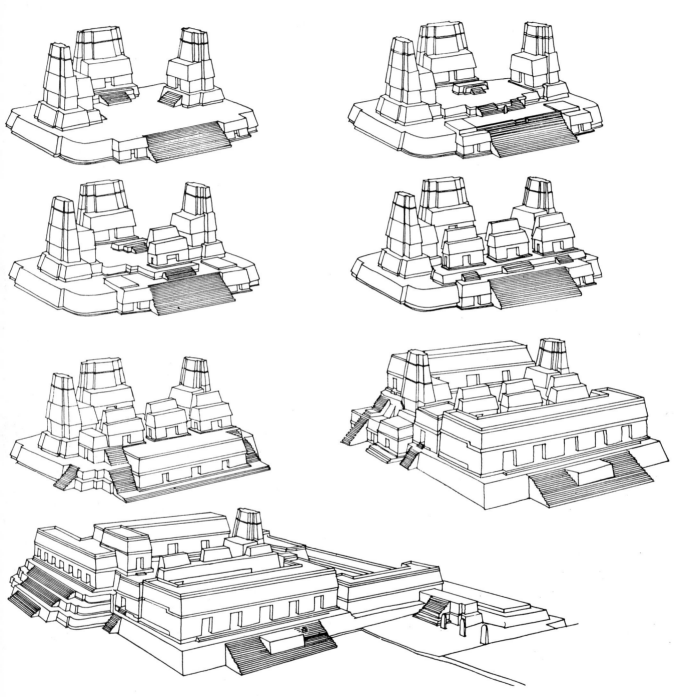

Growth of Group A-V at Uaxactun by successive
superimpositions (after Marquina)

their plastic language was not restricted to such extremes. Their reliefs had their own language and the sculptor-decorators were skilled in creating a successful formal dynamic movement from the compact, static network provided by the large-scale geometrical themes of their key ornaments and masks. Thus their decorative friezes are illuminated by the clever use of an unchanging background contrasting with a sequence of rhythmically flowing and ebbing motifs. This technique of contrast is further echoed by the smooth walls and restless decoration. In the same way the shining white façades accentuate the dark holes of the doorways.

Probably the most extraordinary sculptural discovery of the Maya are the powerful binder moldings which encircle their buildings. Thus the façades of their palaces are divided into two by a band of shadow which accentuates their horizontal movement and endows them with a stability in harmony with the vast perspectives of the landscape. The linear composition of the buildings harmonizes with the natural surroundings and adapts them to the permanent features of their setting. The binder molding represents the unifying factor of the entire work. It creates a hyphen of shadow between the doorways which henceforward participate in the general rhythm of blacks and whites instead of appearing as cells pierced here and there in the naked wall.

The Maya gained their effects by association and contrast. Between the huge façades, their generous proportions radiant in the sunlight, and the tiny, dark, almost oppressive interior spaces, is established a dialectic of architectural symbolism.

The interplay of form and sculpture, based on contrasts and still further accentuated by a skilful use of right angles, does not, however, result in the splendid isolation of the architecture: the palaces are not forbidding. On the contrary, the façades are like mirrors: their dazzling whiteness and luminous friezes magnify the brilliant sun and are in harmony with their surroundings. Opposed to this daylight aspect, however, is their appearance by night; all these buildings have dual personalities. By day they charm and captivate, harmonize with the exterior world and can be termed examples of extrovert art. By night, however, they become introverted, turning in on themselves with their brooding interior spaces.

The Expression of Town-Planning

The Mayan wall, unlike the Gothic, is turned outward. There is a relationship between the solidity of the architecture and the empty spaces of town-planning: the wide esplanades serve to enhance the scale of the solemn creations of the pre-Columbian builders. The impression of backward movement imposed by the terraces and platforms causes the austere rectangles of the buildings to harmonize with the surrounding space. The combinations of this formal syntax surprise by their simplicity. The Maya had recourse to astonishingly balanced means of expression, and the subtle results obtained are no less admirable. Their artificial acropolises do not raise up the buildings so as to cut them off from the world. They form spring-boards whereby the eye passes unconsciously from the natural landscape to the built-up surfaces. There is nothing in common between the Acropolis at Athens, a regal plateau on which is presented in isolation the crowning masterpiece of the Parthenon, and the Mayan platforms with their successive levels relating the artificial world of architecture to the natural world of its setting. There is no break or cleavage resembling the perpendicular cliff of the Acropolis, but a series of ramps, useless for defensive purposes, yet creating a link between the different levels.

In this setting, the stairways obviously occupy an important place: they bring about a flow of wide perspectives among the different levels of what is really a piece of town-planning. Moreover, this use of pedestals of varying heights indicates a very subtle and advanced understanding of the development of architectural elements. The interplay of steps and sills, of stairways and abrupt flights scaling the pyramids endows the space with rhythm. It builds up stresses so that, on the horizontal plane, the concentration of buildings at certain points creates nodal points of intensity. The framework of Mayan cities in no way resembles that of present-day towns. They are not made up of a fairly regular pattern of streets among which an occasional open space gives an essential feeling of repose. On the contrary, the inhabited area is punctuated by more compact groups of buildings.

The combinations of these groups vary from the simplest form of juxtaposition to cleverly arranged complexes. Thus the Palace of the Governor at Uxmal is merely balanced by the small House of the Tortoises, almost at right angles and set slightly back from it. The contrasts of geometrical elements are seldom so plain to the eye. The complex plans are usually on a larger scale. The combination most frequently used by the Maya consists of a fairly large courtyard within a quadrilateral. The cities grew at random by the addition of squares whose empty spaces were bordered by buildings.

This principle, still in course of development in the cities of the Peten, can be confirmed at Copan and is displayed in all its splendor in Puuc architecture. It is already identifiable both at Tikal and Naranjo where the contrasting and balanced groups of temples are formed into vast squares bounded by the vertical accentuation of the pyramids. There are, however, only a few extended buildings capable of producing a real spatial effect. In the cities of Yucatan, these quadrilaterals gain a clearer significance on account of the low lines of the buildings bordering them. Sometimes the courtyards are completely closed, as at the House of the Pigeons at Uxmal, sometimes they are open at the corners, as at the Nunnery. But the most common device is for these complexes, typified by the horizontal lines of the palaces, to be flanked by a high pyramid forming a massive counterpoint. In this case the interplay of contrasts gains its full plastic value, the hollow space of the courtyard answering the projecting element supplied by the trunk of the pyramid.

These planned complexes provide a very impressive architectural experience. The visitor to the courtyard of the Nunnery at Uxmal who enters by the triumphal arch situated on the south side encounters a series of spatial impressions of high quality. Though the approach to the south façade has lost its original attraction because of the ruinous state of the front portion of the building, it is none the less impressive. A long ascent whose gentle slope conceals the north building, though it is, in fact, considerably higher, leads to a wide stairway and thence to the restricted entrance arch which sucks in the visitor and prepares the way for the spatial explosion of the interior court. Once past the threshold of the triumphal arch, one is wholly seized by the completeness of this formal world. The square with its open corners measures 260 by 210 feet and represents one of the highest achievements of the gradual victory won by the Maya in their attempts to make a visual enclosure of outer space, giving it boundaries without enclosing it completely. The side openings offer views down the wings which stimulate the eye, and offer it hidden depths.

Entering through the center of the lowest block one sees to right and left short flights of steps supporting the two side wings, while in front, a great stairway flanked by two galleries seems to snatch up the façade of the north

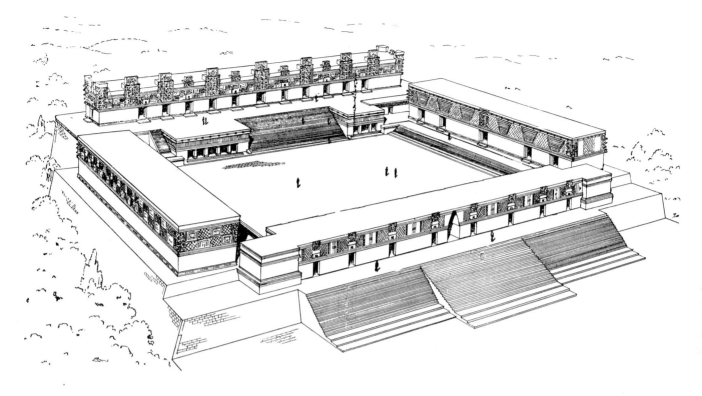

Quadrilateral of the Nunnery at Uxmal (Marquina)

building in an ascending movement. These oblique levels of steps prevent the eye from abruptly hitting a vertical wall, and, thanks to the arrangement of wide ramps, the space expands both sideways and upwards. Furthermore the perspective is accentuated by the trapezoidal plan which contracts towards the rear, so helping to accelerate the spatial movement. Thus the Maya have brought to thrilling life a group of buildings which might easily have appeared static.

Characteristics of Mayan Cities

The Maya carefully arranged the entrance axes of their groups of buildings so as to set off the exterior spaces to best advantage. They also succeeded in endowing the buildings with an exceptional intensity of expression on account of

the wide perspectives requiring a continual approach to the monuments; but they were, on the other hand, unpreoccupied with the idea of traffic. The absence of any form of vehicle or beast of burden made streets unnecessary. Their town-planning, with its rejection of the street system, gave their cities an almost modern look.

From this we should not conclude that there were no wide avenues designed for the passage of processions or for commercial movement. Within the pattern of the cities well-planned roads linked the various nodal points where the concentrations of buildings became thicker. For the Mayan cities were frequently conceived in the same way as our satellite towns, their main centers surrounded at various distances by secondary ones.

179

These towns were real garden cities and it is difficult to picture a more modern formula for town-planning. Their layout is none other than that of the pedestrian precinct with its landscaping and free design, its alternation of esplanades and deep hills, cultivated ground and palm trees and, at Tikal, the Maya even included reservoirs in a plan of remarkable diversity. This is a far cry from the mean towns of the great Eastern civilizations. Cleanliness, coolness and a feeling of space here foreshadow the best developed rules of modern town-planning. For a complete picture of this setting we still have to imagine the palaces and pyramids with their polychrome decoration and their colored stone. Some, at Uxmal, ranged from ivory white to pink, others, at Labna were orange, and, at Chichen Itza, grey with incrustations of black lichen whilst, at Copan, the stone was a dark green.

Outside the cities, the roads formed an important network for commerce. Uxmal was linked to Kabah by one ten miles long and the great triumphal arch at the end of it gave the entrance to the city an air of majestic splendor. A highway over 60 miles long and 30 feet wide, built in three straight sections linked Coba with Yaxuna. This road crossed swamps, often necessitating quite high embankments, for Mayan highways were always perfectly level.

At Palenque the town plan included an underground aqueduct in which the river, diverted from its course, flowed in a vaulted tunnel and, in the same city, a vaulted bridge spanned the water. Finally we must remember the highly decorative role played by the stelae in the cities of the Peten where great consideration was given to their siting. They punctuated the esplanades at the feet of the pyramids, just as, at Copan, the huge monoliths described as altars created points of tension between the buildings and the monumental stairways.

Other elements of town-planning made their appearance with the arrival of the Itzas in Yucatan. These included platforms for dances or sacrifices flanked by staircases, dominated at their summits by the famous plumed serpents' heads.

The Mayan cities display a great variety of plans, but certain distinctive characteristics are apparent in every case. In the right-angled plans on strict north-south axes of Tikal, Nakum, and Ikkum, in the less systematic orientations of Naranjo and Uxmal, the freer outlines of Copan, Palenque and Piedras Negras, in the clearly organic structures of Yaxchilan which are adapted to the broken ground of the banks of the Usumacinta, and at San José in British Honduras, where the great buildings form a group round a natural acropolis, there is always the same use of squares, esplanades and widely deployed exterior spaces.

The marked differences between the plans and layouts of the chief cities, and their variety of style, point to a relative degree of autonomy in the different provinces of Mayan civilization.

The fact that the huts were scattered over a vast area, rendering the distinction between town and country imprecise, explains the basic pacifism of the Maya. These garden cities had no fortifications. Walls appeared only in the final period when the arrival of the Itzas from Chichen disturbed the peaceful inhabitants, infecting them momentarily with the war virus. The league of Mayapan barely succeeded in bringing to a halt this movement of disintegration which was accompanied by constant guerilla warfare between the thirteenth and sixteenth centuries. Tulum, which faces the sea, possesses a late ring of fortifications measuring 1,300 by 460 feet, pierced by five gates, and surrounding the temples and palaces. This section of the city represents no more than the northern sector of a fortress whose walls and defensive systems extend over a half a mile towards the south to embrace the populous quarter of the city.

Population and Toponymy

It is, of course, difficult to estimate the populations of the great Mayan cities at the height of their development. Calculations of this type are always very uncertain; even in the case of peoples and civilizations about which much more is known than the Maya, experts allow a margin of error varying from a third to five times as much as the given figure.

In estimating the population of Uaxactun at 50,000, the Carnegie Institution takes a great risk. In spite of the considerable extension of the huts around the stone buildings in the center, this figure appears enormous. For this reason the computations of Morley who reckoned the populations of Tikal, Copan, Uxmal and Chichen Itza at over 200,000 clearly seem excessive, despite the knowledge that the center of Copan extended over 75 acres with secondary centers several miles distant. The greatest caution should be exercised concerning these calculations; indeed, similar ones regarding Roman or medieval cities also tend to lead us astray.

The conclusions drawn from the importance of the buildings and the need for manual labor are

Plan of the city of Tulum, backed by the Caribbean and surrounded by a strongly fortified wall

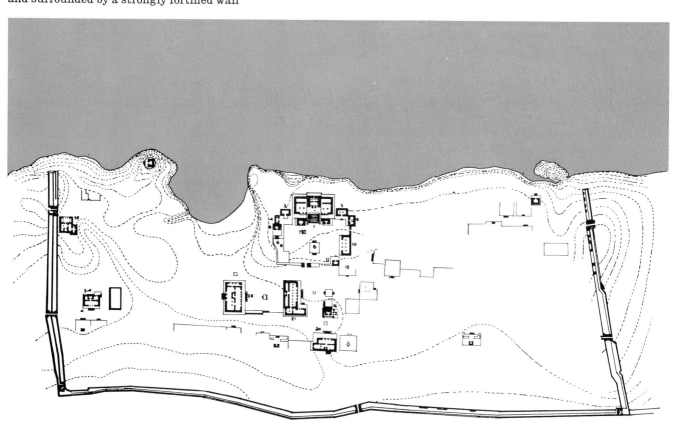

equally inconclusive. But there is no reason to suppose that the Maya did not organize architectural work to coincide with the slack periods of their agricultural activities. In that case, much of their manual labor could easily have been little skilled and this would explain a tendency to mass production.

At the end of this all too brief sketch devoted to the cities, it should be noted that the names of the Mayan towns of the central region almost all date back to the eighteenth and nineteenth centuries, except possibly Copan. For the northern region, on the other hand, texts such as the Chilam Balam provide many of the names of the ancient cities. Of these, the archaeologists have been able to identify Chichen Itza, Uxmal, Mayapan and Coba. Many other names have been lost and replaced by modern topographical designations which, more often than not, have no connection with the ancient ones.

The Death of Mayan Civilization

In the course of this study devoted to Mayan architecture, we have seen the growth of the civilization of this race of builders. Its features have grown more and more distinct despite the mystery which still surrounds many aspects of this continually baffling culture. From an objective examination of their buildings it appears that, although the Maya did not form an empire or a unified nation, they nevertheless possessed various common characteristics: these ranged from the rudiments of technology and economics peculiar to the Central American peoples to fundamentals of culture such as writing and religion. Though their language was not unified throughout their territories, there must have been a Mayan consciousness just as there was a Greek consciousness which can be identified on either side of the Aegean during periods of their most violent internal strife. Most essential of all, they shared the same thought processes. This loosely-bound unity made possible the survival of a strong regional autonomy, evidence of which lies in artistic styles, the dialects of the different provinces, and the development of local cults.

The constructive vigor of this people with their highly developed technical ability, is expressed in the size of their buildings and the number of cities they have left. Their standardized methods and a tendency to prefabrication are liable to give an impression of a despotic, strictly organized world, but the relative freedom of their town-planning indicates a more humane interpretation of the social structure.

Indeed, as in all agrarian cultures, society as a whole rested on the output of the peasant class. The cultivators supported the entire population and their surplus produce served both to provide reserves for the future and to maintain the nobles and craftsmen. The latter were exclusively devoted to works destined for the ruling class. In the country the economy functioned almost entirely in a closed circuit: pottery, tools and houses were made without recourse to external aids. Only luxury goods and materials were subject to exchange among the members of a limited group of traders who worked only for the nobles and the priests. The nobles used exotic products, both for their personal adornment and in the worship of their divinities.

This system ended in power lying in the hands of a religious oligarchy which demanded more and more from the peasants and the bourgeoisie —the group of traders and craftsmen who had begun to travel and acquire a degree of independence. Apparently the break between the upper and lower classes became more marked, although the life of the nobles never grew wholly distinct from that of the peasants. The similarity of their fundamental needs is stressed by the fact that they kept the form of the peasant hut, transposing it into stone, but leaving the basic structure unmodified. Nevertheless, the pressure exerted on the working classes by the exorbitant demands of the intellectual and religious élites created a gulf between the rural population and the mathematicians isolated in their observatory towers.

The balance lay with the craftsmen and traders for, with their knowledge and economic power, they possessed a dynamic force unknown to the peasant farmers. It seems highly likely that they played the leading part in the opposition, killing the goose that had been laying the golden eggs. Thus, a class that had been out of touch with everyday preoccupations, shut up in the pursuit of mathematical speculations out of reach of the common people, allowed itself to be overthrown without knowing how to reply to the threats of the exasperated lower orders.

Only a pretext, however, could give the signal for the liberation of the forces of the amorphous mass of peasants. The force which was to destroy the massive social structure of the Maya came from without. As the result of the great population movements which spread from the high plateaux of the Meza Central, some tribes had been precipitated as far as the isthmus of Tehuantepec, especially on the Pacific coast, where they came up against the northern frontiers of the Mayan world. These migrations had probably begun a century earlier and reached the edge of Mayan territory round about the ninth century A.D.

The Maya were ill prepared to resist this shock because of their natural pacifism and lack of unity. Yet what followed was not a real invasion succeeded by a formal occupation.

It is possible that bands of foreigners penetrated deep into the territories of the central region, endangering the frail balance that had lasted there for several decades. In fact, lack of stability became apparent in two directions:

first there was internal disquiet which favored disorder, then contact with other peoples who brought fresh gods and new forms of worship. The moral shock that results from all invasions and the combined internal crisis arising from these conditions, led quite naturally to a questioning of traditional values.

Revolt then became possible not only against the established political order, but also against the priests with beliefs and rituals whose prestige had so far remained intact. The chief gods were the object of forms of worship too abstruse for the masses to understand and this helped to separate them from the priesthood. The only beliefs that remained untouched were the popular ones centering on the rural divinities of rain and the harvests: the entire set-up of the astronomical calendar became redundant.

For this reason, when the revolt burst out, it swept all before it, spreading like an epidemic. In close on three generations it covered the vast central region. By the end of the ninth century the insurrection of the peasant masses was complete and the priesthood had ceased to exist. All work stopped on stone buildings; they have been discovered uncompleted just as the sculptors left them on the day when their masters were overthrown. The practice of writing died out and the entering of the dates of the sacred calendar was abandoned. The last inscriptions allow us to follow the victorious march of the peasants: at Palenque, 782; Copan, 801; Tikal, 869 and so on.

Contrary to what the archaeologists believed until quite recently, the cities were not abandoned. At Piedras Negras, Yaxchilan, Bonampak and Palenque, only the representations of high priests on stelae and in paintings were mutilated; their eyes were obliterated, the monoliths thrown to the ground, and the stucco heads broken off. The palaces, however, were not abandoned: they merely ceased to be maintained and soon fell into ruin. Proof of the occupation of these stone buildings by the peasants lies in the fact that numerous grindstones used for maize have been found on the staircases and in the chambers.

In the central region, cultural life came to an end before 900. In Yucatan, though the manifestations of pure Mayan culture ceased shortly afterwards, since the last dates recorded at Chichen and Uxmal are 909, the revolution was apparently less violent; there had already been signs of an early break with the ideas of the southern part of the country about the middle of the sixth century when new styles appeared.

Soon, however, a fresh invasion began in the north of Mayan territory. The revolutionary movement favored the penetration of a wave of migrants that spread along the Atlantic shore of the Gulf. Amongst them were the people of Tula; driven onwards by other invaders from the north, they crossed the coastal forests of Chiapas, and came to rest after a journey of nearly 600 miles at Chichen Itza. These new arrivals, the Itzas, gave rise to the unifying renaissance of Mayan-Toltec culture, signs of which can be found at Uxmal in the motif of the plumed serpent, added to the frieze of the western wing of the Nunnery, and at Tulum in the columns bearing the effigy of Quetzelcoatl-Kukulkan.

The hegemony of the Itzas, however, lasted for no more than two centuries, roughly from 985 to 1185. Disintegration followed. Guerilla warfare between the tribes hastened the ruin of Mayan culture which had none the less succeeded in assimilating its masters of Mexican origin and caused them to forget their gods. This mayanization continued during the general decay of culture. Only a small, degenerate élite maintained the religious writings and the traditions of the ancient civilization. These were the books which Bishop Landa ordered to be burnt in the square of Mani in the first years of the Spanish Conquest.

The southern part of the Mayan world had returned to its primitive state before the arrival of the Spaniards and, though a semblance of autonomous culture survived in the north, the old stone cities had already fallen into ruin in the thirteenth and fourteenth centuries.

The entire population once more inhabited the unchanging houses of thatch and pisé. The Mayan world had turned full circle and returned to its point of departure. The vital cycle of this civilization was ended at the very moment when the ships of Cortes reached the coast of Yucatan. The handful of adventurers who conquered the country between 1525 and 1541 met with a dead culture.

Nevertheless, the inheritance of Mayan architecture conveys to the twentieth century the evidence of a dazzling past and a glorious, subtle civilization. Similarly, Mayan town-planning is capable of teaching present-day architects by its sense of space, its generosity and the miraculous harmony it was able to create between the works of man and nature. What greater destiny could have been claimed by these stone age tribes, who have shown us how to build garden cities in the heart of the hostile forest and who erected the glowing façades of their strangely modern-looking palaces with the help of productive techniques that were to be rediscovered in the New World exactly a thousand years later?

The legacy of the Maya, revealed thanks to the patience of the archaeologists, is a heritage of beauty, light and balance which moves us as deeply as the work of our own ancestors, because we are now more than ever able to appreciate its humane and splendid message.

Chronological Table

Dates	Mexico	Tikal	Copan	Palenque
200	Civilization of Teotihuacan I Cholula II Monte Alban III Xochicalco I	Red stele (290)		
300	Teotihuacan II Xochicalco II			
400		Stele 18 (416) Basle wooden relief (481)	Stele 24 (485)	
500	Teotihuacan II Cholula III		Ball-Court (514) Hieroglyphic Staircases (545)	Temple of the Foliated Cross (536)
600	Tajin			Temple of the Sun (642) Great Palace (672) Pyramid of the Inscriptions (692)
700			Stele B (732) Staircase stele (757) Spectators' Gallery (771)	Palace Tower (783)
800	Teotihuacan IV Cholula IV The Mixtecs	Last date: Stele 11 (869)	Last date: Altar G. (801)	
900	Civilization of the Toltecs at Tula Xochicalco IV Monte Alban IV			
1000	The Aztecs I New Cholula I			
1100	Fall of Tula (1168)			

Yucatan	Uxmal	Chichen Itza	Historical Landmarks	Dates
				200
			Caracalla (211) The Sassanides (227) Invasions of Franks, Huns and Goths	
				300
			Constantine (312) The Huns in China Theodosius (379) Honorius (395)	
				400
Calakbal (406) Dzibilchaltun (485)		Foundation (?) 433	War between Attila and Theodosius II (441) Clovis (482) Theodoric in Italy (489)	
				500
Beginning of the Chenes, Rio Bec and Puuc styles (c.550)			Justinian (527) The Lombards in Italy (568)	
				600
	Ball-Court (649)		Heraclius (610) T'ang Dynasty in China (618) Start of the Arab Conquest (632)	
				700
	Pyramid of the Magician?		Defeat of the Mohammedans at Poitiers (732) Foundation of Baghdad (762) Charlemagne (768)	
				800
Date at Labna: 869 Date at Kabah: 879	Palace of the Governor?		The Vikings in Ireland (830) Emergence of the Khmers	
				900
	Last date: Nunnery (909)	Last Mayan date: Caracol (909) Mexican invasion (967)	End of the T'ang Dynasty (908) The Sung Dynasty in China (960) Otto I (962)	
				1000
		League of Mayapan (1007)	The Normans in Italy (1029) and in England (1066) First Crusade (1099)	
				1100
		Collapse of Mexican domination (1185)	S'rutavarman builds Angkor Vat Genghis Khan at the head of the Mongols	

Bibliography

Monographs

Gallenkamp, C.
Les Mayas; la découverte d'une civilisation perdue. Paris, Payot 1961

Krickeberg, W.
Las Antiguas Culturas Mexicanas. Mexico, Fondo de Cultura Economica 1961

Mariscal, F.
Estudio Arquitectonico de las Ruinas Mayas. Mexico, Secretaria de Educacion Publica 1928

Marquina, I.
Estudio Arquitectonico Comparativo de los Monumientos Arqueologicos de Mexico. Mexico, Secretaria de Educacion Publica 1928

Marquina, I.
Arquitectura Prehispanica. Mexico, Memorias del Instituto Nacional de Antropologia e Historia 1951

Morley, S.
La Civilizacion Maya. Mexico, Fondo de Cultura Economica 1961

Muelleried, F.
Contribucion a la Geologia de Mexico y Noroeste de La America Central. Universidad Nacional Autonoma de Mexico 1945

Proskouriakoff, T.
An Album of Maya Architecture. Washington, Carnegie Institution 1946

Proskouriakoff, T.
A Study of Classic Maya Sculpture. Washington, Carnegie Institution 1951

Rivet, P.
Cités Mayas. Paris, Albert Guillot 1954

Ruz Lhuillier, A.
La Civilizacion de los Antiguos Mayas. Mexico, Instituto Nacional de Antropologia e Historia 1963

Ruz Lhuillier, A.
Influencias Mexicanas sobre los Mayas. Wenner-Gren Foundation for Anthropological Research 1962

Ruz Lhuillier, A.
Universalidad, Singularidad y Pluridad del Arte Maya. Merida 1950

Spinden, H.
A Study of Maya Art. Peabody Museum of Archeology and Ethnology, Memoirs Vol. VI, Cambridge 1913

Termer, F.
Die Halbinsel Yucatan. Petermanns Geographische Mitteilungen, Erg. Heft 253, Gotha 1954

Thompson, E.
Grandeur et décadence de la civilisation maya. Paris, Payot 1958

Toscano, S.
Arte Precolombino de Mexico y de la America central. Universidad Nacional Autonoma de Mexico 1952

Tozzer, A.
Chichen Itza and its Cenote of Sacrifice. Peabody Museum of Archeology and Ethnology, Memoirs, Vol. XI-XII, Cambridge 1957

Wolf, E.
Peuples et Civilisations de l'Amérique centrale. Payot 1962

General Works

Estado actual de los Principales Edificios Arqueologicos de Mexico. Mexico, Secretaria de Educacion Publica 1928

Estudios de Cultura Maya, Vol. I and II, Universidad Nacional Autonoma de Mexico 1961-1962

Les Grands Architectes (Chapter by Geneviève Bonnefoi).
Paris, Mazenod 1958

Official guides of INAH (Palenque, Tulum, Uxmal,
Chichen Itza, Ciudades Mayas, etc.)

Histoire de l'Art, Vol. I, Encyclopédie de la Pléiade
(Chapter by Raoul d'Harcourt). Paris, Gallimard 1961

Histoire universelle, Vol. II, Encyclopédie de la Pléiade
(Chapter by Jacques Soustelle). Paris, Gallimard 1957

Miscellanea Paul Rivet (Chapters by Alberto Ruz, George
Kubler, Franz Termer, Chevalier and Huguet). Universidad Nacional Autonoma de Mexico 1958

Publicaciones del Idach, Antropologia e Historia de
Guatemala, Ministerio de Educacion Publica, 1951 et seqq.

Les Religions Amérindiennes (Chapter by W. Krickeberg).
Paris, Payot 1962

Interviews recorded by the author

Documentaries from the series "L'Epopée des Civilisations", recorded in Mexico in 1962 with:

Ignacio Bernal, Assistant Director, Instituto Nacional de
Antropologia e Historia, Mexico, ("Le fond culturel
commun de l'Amérique moyenne")

Luis Lorenzo, Professor of American Prehistory, INAH,
Mexico, ("L'origine du peuplement américain")

Alberto Ruz Lhuillier, Director of Studies of Mayan
Culture, Professor of the Universidad Nacional Autonoma de Mexico, ("Le déclin de la civilisation maya"
and "La découverte de la crypte de Palenque")

Acknowledgements

The author wishes to express his deep gratitude to Professor Alberto Ruz Lhuillier of the Universidad Nacional
Autonoma in Mexico City, Director of Studies of Mayan
Culture, for his great kindness in reading through the
manuscript, giving him invaluable advice, and communicating to him a variety of hitherto unpublished facts.

He is also grateful to all those who have enabled him to
complete his photographic documentation of the sites on
which he was prevented from working himself, particularly
those beyond the frontiers of Mexico. Fifteen of the first
set of reproductions were not taken by the author, but are
credited as follows:

pp. 21, 23, 30, by Alfred Ayotte, Montreal.

pp. 22, 24, 31, by Charles Bonnet, Geneva.

pp. 28, 29, 32, by Mme. Hélène Hoppenot, Paris.

pp. 26, 33, by Jean-Pierre Ivanov, Paris.

p. 25, by Peter Moeschlin, Basle.

p. 37, by Hamilton Wright, Mexico.

p. 43, by the Instituto Nacional de Antropologia e
Historia, Mexico City.

Thanks are also due to the Mexican authorities, in particular the Mexican Tourist Board and the Instituto
Nacional de Antropologia e Historia, for their help and
kind support throughout the author's stay in Mexico.

Finally he wishes to stress the important facilities
accorded by the Sabena airline of Brussels on the line
Brussels – Montreal – Mexico, and by the Mexicana de
Aviacion on flights between Mexico City and Merida. To
these companies he offers his special thanks.

INDEX Numerals in black type refer to illustrations